Grow 'Em Right
A Guide to Creating Habitat and Food Plots

by

Neil and Craig Dougherty

Edited by

Aaron Alsheimer and Patrick Durkin

© 2003 by
Neil and Craig Dougherty

All rights reserved. No portion of this publication may be reproduced or transmitted in any form or by any means, electronic or mechanical, including photocopy, recording, or any information storage and retrieval system, without permission in writing from the author, except by a reviewer who may quote brief passages in a critical article or review to be printed in a magazine or newspaper, or electronically transmitted on radio or television.

Published by
NorthCountry Whitetails LLC
P.O. Box 925
Fairport, New York 14450

Photos by NorthCountry Whitetails unless otherwsie noted.

ISBN: 0-9729356-0-6

Library of Congress Control Number: 2003103411

Printed in the United States of America

LIMIT OF LIABILITY/DISCLAIMER OF WARRANTY: THE PUBLISHER AND AUTHORS HAVE USED THEIR BEST EFFORTS IN PREPARING THIS BOOK. THE PUBLISHER AND AUTHORS MAKE NO REPRESENTATIONS OR WARRANTIES WITH RESPECT TO THE ACCURACY OR COMPLETENESS OF THE CONTENTS OF THIS BOOK AND SPECIFICALLY DISCLAIM ANY IMPLIED WARRANTIES OF MERCHANTABILITY OR FITNESS FOR A PARTICULAR PURPOSE. THERE ARE NO WARRANTIES WHICH EXTEND BEYOND THE DESCRIPTIONS CONTAINED IN THIS PARAGRAPH. NO WARRANTY MAY BE CREATED OR EXTENDED BY SALES REPRESENTATIVES OR WRITTEN SALES MATERIALS. THE ACCURACY AND COMPLETENESS OF THE INFORMATION PROVIDED HEREIN AND THE OPINIONS STATED HEREIN ARE NOT GUARANTEED OR WARRANTED TO PRODUCE ANY PARTICULAR RESULTS, AND THE ADVICE AND STRATEGIES CONTAINED HEREIN MAY NOT BE SUITABLE FOR EVERY INDIVIDUAL. NEITHER THE PUBLISHER NOR AUTHORS SHALL BE LIABLE FOR ANY LOSS OF PROFIT OR ANY OTHER COMMERCIAL DAMAGES, INCLUDING BUT NOT LIMITED TO SPECIAL, INCIDENTAL, CONSEQUENTIAL, OR OTHER DAMAGES.

DEDICATION

To

"Kindred Spirits"

and all

who gather

there.

"Conservation means harmony between men and land. When land does well for its owner and the owner does well by his land, when both end up better by reason of their partnership, we have conservation."

— Aldo Leopold

Contents

Dedication iii

Acknowledgments vi

Foreword by Charlie Alsheimer vii

Chapter I	Why We Wrote This Book	13
Chapter II	Getting Started...	
	Make a Commitment, Develop a Plan	31
Chapter III	A Chainsaw is a Deer's Best Friend	49
Chapter IV	Property Access - Preventing and Creating	67
Chapter V	Logging Roads & Clearings	87
Chapter VI	Creating Sanctuaries	101
Chapter VII	Woods Working - TSI	111
Chapter VIII	Logging On	123
Chapter IX	Food Plots for Feeding	133
Chapter X	Food Plots for Hunting	151
Chapter XI	Big Toys for Big Boys (and Girls)	175
Chapter XII	Selecting Cultivars for the Food Plot	189
Chapter XIII	Quality Deer Hunting	207
Chapter XIV	Getting Started	225

Appendix A 229

Appendix B 231

Index 242

ACKNOWLEDGMENTS

Many people assisted us with this book. They are all important to us and are deserving of our heartfelt thanks. They appear below in alphabetical order:

Aaron Alsheimer
Chris Asplundh
Kathy Balbierer and Kacey
Randy Bridge
Willis Brown
Dave & Beth Buckley
Joe Byers
Bobby Cole
Jill & Peter Crawford
Darrell Daigre
Bob "Gramps" Dougherty
Janet Dougherty
Patrick Durkin
Peter & Kate Fiduccia
Bob Foulkrod
Mike Griffin
Ryan Kerfien
Brian Murphy
Laura & Charlie Palmer
Dave Reitano
Sharon Scholl and Erin
Jeff, Wayne & Steve Storie
Carl Whittier
Dr. Grant Woods

and

Charlie Alsheimer
for
Leading the Way

FOREWORD

Life is full of beginnings, with each new undertaking adding to life's total. In assessing my quarter-century as an outdoor communicator, I continually reflect on what has made my life a blessing beyond measure. Each new dawn, wildlife encounter and connection with another kindred spirit has played a significant role in my special journey.

I was born and raised on a farm in New York's Southern-Tier potato region. From an early age I had a bond with nature. Early on, this was manifested through hunting, which in time was enhanced by becoming a nature photographer and outdoor writer. It was only after I passed age 40 that I truly came to understand what stewarding the land is all about. In 1989 I traveled to South Texas to hunt and photograph. While there I met the legendary Al Brothers, considered by many to be the father of the Quality Deer Management movement. He encouraged me to try and implement the QDM concept on my farm. I took Brothers' words to heart and changed the way I had been managing the property.

For more than 10 years, I've been immersed in QDM. I admit there were times in the beginning I wasn't sure I was doing the right thing. This stemmed from skeptical reactions from fellow New Yorkers and the program's slow pace.

Traditions die hard in the Northeast and the thought of managing land for quality deer, habitat and enjoyment was not an idea embraced by many New Yorkers in the early 1990s. Despite the drawbacks, I kept the vision and kept moving forward, thanks in large part to close friends and the successes we saw.

For years, I dreamed of the day quality bucks would walk the fields of western New York. It took time, but the day has arrived, thanks in large part to the vision of many like-minded individuals and landowners in our area. .Two of the most inspirational have been my country neighbors and friends, Craig and Neil Dougherty.

Nearly a decade ago, I met Craig at the urging of fellow outdoor writer Bob Robb. At the time, I knew Craig as one of the "heavy hitters" in the hunting industry, but didn't know he owned property a scant seven air miles from my farm.

So, one sunny spring morning I drove from my farm to the top of the Catatunk, a forested hilltop region that sits on one of the highest points in Steuben County, New York. Craig and I had agreed to meet at his place after a morning of hunting spring gobblers on our respective properties. After the usual greetings we sat in lawn chairs and sipped coffee next to his pop-up camper, while looking out over the beautiful Canisteo Valley.

The meeting was enlightening. For the better part of three hours we discussed the outdoor industry, hunting, our families and what we were doing with our properties. At the time I was a couple of years into managing our deer under the relatively new QDM concept that Al Brothers laid upon my heart in 1989. During our conversation, I learned Craig owned 150 acres, but had visions of adding more acreage and, as he put it, "Doing something more productive with it than just using it as a place to hunt."

By the nature of the questions he asked that morning, I could tell he was intrigued by what I was trying to do with my property. Over the next three years, Craig, Neil and I had many fireside discussions concerning the pros and cons of quality deer management, as well as how to develop a property for both wildlife and hunting. It was obvious Craig and his son were excited by the prospects of what they could accomplish on their property, which they called "Kindred Spirits."

Over time they purchased more land, built a beautiful cabin, erected a conference center, and put their dream into motion. They involved wildlife/land management experts like Dave and Beth Buckley of West Valley, N.Y., Dr. Grant Woods and bowhunting expert Bob Foulkrod in an attempt to flatten the wildlife-management learning curve, and set up a state-of-the-art program. NorthCountry Whitetails Habitat Development and Hunting Demo Center was taking shape. As I watched what was growing, it was easy to see the Doughertys had fallen in love with the concept of land management and quality deer hunting.

The result is that their vision has become a reality. It has taken time, but through much sweat and effort they've been able to put together a model 500-acre property that benefits both hunters and landowners.

It's safe to say their NorthCountry Whitetails Demo Center, located in rural Steuben County in New York, is a unique concept. In fact, with its tour program and conference center activities, it is the only one of its kind in the north, to my knowledge. The practices and techniques they've developed have become the envy of nearly every landowner and hunter who has been introduced to their style of land/wildlife management. Hundreds have learned the "how-to's" of habitat management and food plots from visiting the operation.

Now they've taken their program to the next level by sharing how they did it in the book you are holding. If you are looking for a "how-to" volume on creating a white-tailed deer Mecca that benefits habitat, all wildlife and the hunter, this is it. If you are struggling with how to turn your land or hunting lease into something better, this book can show you how to do it. In short, this book is a down-to-earth, step-by-step volume on how to cut your losses and reap big gains in the shortest length of time.

For too long, many have viewed the concept of land development and quality deer management as something complicated. Although it can be difficult if not done properly, pulling it off is not rocket science. *Grow 'Em Right: A Guide to Creating Habitat and Food Plots*, will show you how to obtain the results you are dreaming about in the least amount of time.

So, sit back and let the Doughertys lead you on a cutting-edge wildlife journey, the likes of which you've probably never experienced. If you're like me, you'll be a better steward for having done so.

Charlie Alsheimer
Northern Field Editor
Deer and Deer Hunting *magazine*

Photo by Charles J. Alsheimer

Photo by Charles J. Alsheimer

Chapter I

Why We Wrote This Book

Neil and Steve charged through the cabin door, their eyes as big as saucers. They couldn't wait to tell Craig and bowhunting legend Bob Foulkrod what they had just seen. Dressed in T-shirts for the unseasonably hot weather, they had spent midday scouting a seldom-hunted area. They were about 75 yards apart in thick cover, but each got a close look at a majestic white-tailed buck as it dogged a doe. The buck's 20-inch spread made them confident it would make "the book" with plenty to spare. This deer was the biggest buck either had seen on the property. It wasn't many years ago that any buck got the boys in this Steuben County, New York, camp excited. But things have improved dramatically since then.

Minutes later, the four hunters held a meeting to craft a hunting strategy. The encounter with the big buck occurred in terrain near "The Hole," a steep, thick semi-sanctuary they rarely hunted. Rather than risk spooking the buck from the area, they set up stands near the site's perimeter, hoping to catch him coming out after does.

Neil Dougherty got this 136 Pope-and-Young buck five years after he and his father, Craig, decided to practice "quality deer hunting" on their property in Steuben County, New York. Neil and Craig progressed from shooting spikes, forkhorns and small 6-pointers to record-book deer. They now routinely see bucks like this one.

For the rest of the weekend, the hunters focused their efforts on "The Big One." Gone was the need for instant success. They tried to understand their quarry's habits and get in position for a shot. On the weekend's last sit, Neil spotted the buck again as it left The Hole with its nose to the ground. The buck obviously had does on the brain.

The deer walked past Neil's stand about 40 yards upwind, hit a clover-covered logging road, and turned uphill. It was moving steadily along the road and would pass through a shooting lane at about 30 yards. When the buck walked behind a mass of grape vines, Neil drew his bow. The release was true and the arrow found its mark.

Why We Wrote this Book

Neil waited a half-hour until he could stand the suspense no longer. After climbing down and investigating, he found his blood-covered arrow. Minutes later, 75 yards along the trail, he spotted brown, and then the antlers. The 136 Pope-and-Young buck lay still in the leaves. Neil couldn't wait to tell everyone. Craig, Neil's father, had already departed because of a business obligation. He heard the story via his cell phone while at Tampa's airport.

Since that day, Neil's buck has been written about in several hunting magazines, not because of its size — it's not outstanding, as book-bucks go — but because of what it represents. Neil's big buck came after eight years of intensive quality deer hunting and habitat-development work at NorthCountry's 500-acre property in hunter-dense Steuben County, New York. Neil's buck represented a defining moment. We had taken a trophy buck from our property, a feat we once thought impossible. Our habitat development and quality deer-hunting program was working! Neil's buck was a perfect case-study of how to improve deer hunting on a typical woodland property.

The Demo Center is Born

Today, the same property — which routinely produces record-book bucks — is more than a hunting property. It has been converted into the only "Habitat and Hunting Development Demo Center" of its kind in the northern United States. It is 500 acres of prime deer range, much of it created through habitat-development projects over the past 10 years. It is also BioLogic's Northern Research Facility, with acres of BioLogic test plots and experimental food-plot blends. Best of all, it offers educational programs to the public.

The center has been featured on television programs and written about in newspapers and magazines. With more than 50 percent of all licensed deer hunters living within an eight-hour drive of the facility, it has more than its share of visitors.

This book is organized around the Demo Center's tours. It is not about theory. It's about practice. It's about what has worked for us, and what we know will work for you. Our book, like our tours, emphasizes a balanced approach to quality deer hunting and habitat development. It's about total property management, not just food plots. It's about creating quality wildlife habitat and quality deer hunting. It addresses the everyday problems and

Neil Dougherty, fourth from right, discusses food plots with a tour group visiting the NorthCountry Demo Center. Each year Neil leads hundreds of visitors through the 500-acre property. Many are landowners setting out on their own quality deer hunting endeavor.

Why We Wrote this Book

questions of the thousands of habitat-development enthusiasts we talk with each year. These questions include:

1 "What can I do about trespassers?"

2 "How do I get my neighbors to cooperate?"

3 "How can I set up food plots for better bowhunting opportunities?"

4 "How do I set up a sanctuary?"

5 "What can I expect if I clearcut a patch of woods?"

6 "How much lime and fertilizer should I apply, and how should I apply it?"

This book discusses what works, what doesn't, and how we progressed from rookie habitat managers to creators of one of the North's finest examples of whitetail range.

Creating Quality Whitetail Hunting

This book is also about creating quality whitetail hunting. In the late 1980s, we dreamed about having our own place to hunt whitetails. By the early 1990s, we dreamed of seeing trophy bucks on our property. By 2000, our dreams had become reality.

By the late 1990s, we had also met thousands of deer enthusiasts with identical dreams. They visit our facility almost every weekend, visit our Web site (www.NorthCountryWhitetails.com), and attend Neil's public seminars. They constantly ask: "I've always dreamed about having quality deer hunting. How do I make it happen?"

These Steuben County trophies were taken within 48 hours of each other from two separate New York properties, both of which follow practices outlined in this book. Ten years ago, a photo like this would have shown forkhorns, 6-pointers and maybe a basket 8-pointer. Today, whitetails this size are seen regularly on our properties.

Above all, this book strives to help others realize their dreams. We believe a quality deer hunting experience is within the grasp of almost anyone who works hard, is willing to learn, and wants it enough to dare to dream. Our Demo-Center tours and seminars have helped thousands of deer hunters get closer to living their dream.

The Book is Based on Experience

We've tried every plan and technique we write about in this book. This book is not a review of scientific research or a compilation of telephone interviews with experts. It is a hands-on book about hands-on projects and practices. But, make no mistake: It's

Why We Wrote this Book

not all about what we "learned the hard way." Far from it. Since the early 1990s, we have worked with the top experts in the business. Each of them has spent lots of time at the Demo Center, working and hunting beside us. You can see the influence of our group of experts on projects all over the Demo Center. We know of no other property that has received so much attention from so many leaders in hunting and wildlife management. Each brings a specific set of knowledge and skills, and each complements the others.

Neil took these two "book bucks" within 24 hours of each other from the same food plot. The smaller buck was taken with a brand-new bow on the last afternoon of New York's archery season. The bigger buck was taken the next day during the first afternoon of gun season. Both bucks were checking out does feeding on snow-covered brassica.

Leading Experts in the Field

Charlie Alsheimer, arguably one of the best whitetail photographers in North America, is an expert on deer behavior. He spends lots of time with a herd of white-tailed deer he keeps on his Steuben County farm in New York. When he's not photographing and studying whitetails, Charlie is busy writing about them.

Photo by Charles J. Alsheimer

In short, we have been blessed to work with some of the best hunting and habitat-development professionals in the country. They have been our mentors. Our good friend Charles Alsheimer, who started us down the quality deer-hunting path, is one of North America's top white-tailed deer behaviorists and, arguably, its best whitetail photographer. Charlie has been a pioneer in quality deer management in the North, and is responsible for showing thousands of hunters the way with his one-man multi-media shows. He also reaches thousands of hunters with his spectacular book *Quality Deer Management: The Basics and Beyond*. Many habitat projects at our Demo Center were done with Charlie's help. He has been a source of encouragement, helping us "stay the course" since the early 1990s, years when we weren't always confident of our new approach. We continue to conduct research together and exchange information daily.

Dr. Grant Woods, head of Mossy Oak's BioLogic research team, has contributed immeasurably to NorthCountry's understanding of deer nutrition and all growing things. Dr. Woods manages hun-

Why We Wrote this Book

dreds of thousand of acres of wildlife properties for his clients, some of whom run the world's finest hunting operations.

Our facility has used BioLogic food-plot forages for years. As a result, we now operate BioLogic's Northern Research Facility. We experiment with new blends as BioLogic continues to develop and improve forages for diverse climates and conditions across the nation.

Dr. Grant Woods manages hundreds of thousands of acres of deer habitat for his clients in North America. He directs all research activities at BioLogic's Northern Research Facility. This brassica leaf comes from a patented strain developed by Wrightson Seed of New Zealand.

Dr. Woods helped us develop high-quality food plots on marginal soils in severe Northern climatic conditions. Our food plots are nothing short of spectacular, and have paid big dividends in terms of quality deer and hunting. Dr. Woods directs, and Neil manages, all of the forage research on the facility.

Dave and Beth Buckley, friends from western New York, are pioneers in habitat development. They are part of a rare group of individuals who have been doing this 30 or more years. They are willing teachers and stewards of the land. Their property is a model of habitat development. The Buckleys helped enormously to develop the facility during its early years. Their advice started us on

Dave and Beth Buckley are naturalists who have been creating quality deer habitat more than 30 years. They started the Doughertys down the habitat-development path in the early 1990s, and continue to offer them expert advice.

the correct path and kept us there ever since. We always learn something from the Buckleys when we hit the field together.

Bob Foulkrod is a regular at our Demo Center and hunts the property whenever he can. Bob has been a hunting mentor to Neil since he was old enough to draw a bow. As thousands know, Bob is the ultimate bowhunting machine. His occupation as a professional hunter — almost always in front of a camera — requires proficiency in hunting new terrain. He is the master of reading property and setting up for a kill. He has greatly assisted Neil in putting together world-class hunting setups at the Demo Center. These setups, and other hunting strategies from our team of experts, can be viewed by those who visit the NorthCountry Whitetails Demo Center.

Why We Wrote this Book

Bob Foulkrod makes his living by bowhunting. He is considered by many deer hunters to be the best in the business at reading terrain and setting up effective stand sites. He has seen it all, learning something from every one of his thousands of hunts. Many hunting setups at the Demo Center were created by Bob, Neil and Charlie Alsheimer.

This book's authors are a father-son team with a shared passion for hunting and habitat development. Their skills and experiences, while unique, are highly complementary. Craig's background is in research and education. In fact, he was a teacher and university professor for more than a dozen years.

Another of Craig's passions is business and organizational development, especially in the hunting industry. For more than 20 years he has been involved in hunter education, combating antihunters, and growing the sports of archery and bowhunting. He serves as vice chairman of the Fred Bear Equipment Co., and is a member of the Archery Trade Association's board of directors. He is also chairman of the ATA's Bowhunting Preservation Alliance.

Bob Foulkrod, Neil Dougherty and Charlie Alsheimer discuss stand-location strategies at NorthCountry's Demo Center. Visitors to the center see this exact setup and others conceived by the pros. Neil, shown here in the center, presents this setup and others to the public in his magazine articles and hunting seminars.

He is on a first-name basis with most of the big names in the hunting industry, and has worked on projects with many of them.

Neil has grown up around the hunting industry's leaders. As a youngster, he shared campfires with the likes of Bob Foulkrod, Chuck Adams, Toxey Haas and Cuz Strickland. During and after college, he was lucky enough to be mentored while working side by side professionals like Alsheimer and Dr. Woods. In short, Neil has been trained by the best of the best, and it shows in his work.

In addition to running the NorthCountry Whitetails Demo Center, Neil presents about 100 seminars across the country each year. He also writes for several outdoor magazines, and appears

Why We Wrote this Book

frequently on television. He consults landowners across the United States, and still finds time to hunt, which remains his passion. As one of the country's outstanding young hunters, Neil is known best for his ability to use his training and sixth sense to help other hunters find success.

Together, the authors have built an organization — NorthCountry Whitetails — that's dedicated to providing the products, services and education necessary to experience quality deer hunting through habitat development.

• •
We have taken hundreds of people through our outdoors classroom. But we realize not everyone can visit the Demo Center. This book brings the center to our readers.
• •

The results of countless years of learning and teaching by the best deer and hunting experts in the world can be viewed by the public at our Demo Center. The same information is also found in the pages ahead. In our opinion, a better group of well-rounded experts — each with the goal of educating the public about quality deer hunting and habitat management — has never before been assembled.

Our Mission is Education

Our decision to open the Demo Center and invite the public inside for tours, "demo days" and workshops did not come lightly. It's one thing to write articles about our projects and appear on television occasionally, but it's another to invite public participation. We value our privacy and knew the human traffic required

The NorthCountry Whitetails habitat development tour covers about six miles and lasts about four hours. The tractor-drawn tram allows visitors to relax and enjoy while learning basic and advanced habitat concepts. It stops at about 20 demo areas, including habitat projects, food plots and hunting setups.

to share our knowledge and passion for habitat development would probably affect the hunting we cherish. However, the joy of seeing others move closer to realizing their dreams has become an important part of our lives. We are lucky to have learned from the best in the country, and believe others should have the same chance. We share our knowledge and help others develop successful programs. And we do mean successful! Since the early 1990s, every aspect of our hunting experience has improved, and the age structure and size of the deer on our property has increased. Friends and followers of the methods in this book experience similar success.

All Demo Center land is free range. It contains no pens or deer-proof fenced enclosures. We started with 150 acres and now

Why We Wrote this Book

control more than 500 acres. The neighbors on all sides of the Demo Center hunt, but not everyone subscribes to quality deer hunting practices. In fact, one group would be considered poor hunting neighbors. But that's the world we live in, and it's probably similar to your world, too.

We have brought hundreds of people through our outdoors classroom, but we realize not everyone can visit the Demo Center. This book is designed to bring the Demo Center to you. A tour through the habitat-development Demo Center lasts about four hours and includes stops at about 20 sites, each illustrating a unique habitat-development concept. This book is organized

• •
The following chapters will help you avoid mistakes commonly made by landowners. If you follow the lessons of this book, you will be successful, but in half the time it took us.
• •

along the same lines. Each chapter is set in one of our habitat-demo areas, and we encourage you to mentally place yourselves on our demo tour. In essence, this book is a "virtual" tour of NorthCountry Whitetails' Demo Center. Each chapter places you in an outdoors environment where you will learn a new aspect of habitat development and/or quality deer hunting.

This Book: The Demo Center and More

When we started our habitat project, no books like this were available. We read some academic, research-oriented textbooks, but few dealt with habitat development, especially in the North. Our mentors helped chart our way and kept us from making too many big mistakes. Our property didn't come with a handbook or owner's manual. We made mistakes, as everyone does, but we learned from all of them. We hope the following chapters help you avoid common mistakes made by landowners in the early stages of their habitat-development journey. We hope the chapters motivate you, as well. We hope to start you on the path, or perhaps accelerate your progress, by sharing our knowledge and experience. We learned from our mentors, our endless research, and plenty of trial and error. Habitat development is not rocket science, but even today few "hands-on" materials exist in printed form. If you follow the lessons of this book, you too will be successful — but in half the time it took us.

Since starting the Demo Center tours, we have been thrilled with the public's response. Most of our "graduates" left the Demo

Craig and Neil Dougherty with Craig's 150-plus buck taken on the NorthCountry Whitetails' Demo Center in 2002. Ten years before, bucks like this one were only a dream for the father-son team.

Why We Wrote this Book

Center feeling motivated, and have undertaken habitat-management programs of their own. They call and e-mail us year-round with questions and success stories. Virtually everyone who tours our property can relate it to their own.

We hope this book will reach you in a similar way. We want you to envision yourself, your buddies and your property in the pages ahead.

We hope you carry this book in your backpack or on the dashboard of your pickup truck. Keep it handy for reference. Consult it often, and get copies for your friends and neighbors. It's a book to be used repeatedly. It should not be put on the shelf to collect dust. Follow it closely, and your dream of creating quality hunting and white-tailed deer habitat will become a reality.

While Neil's trophy whitetail was a defining moment in our habitat-development journey, it was not the most important moment. That moment came about 1990 when we decided to do something about the mediocre deer hunting we had long experienced. We hope this book helps create that moment for you.

So, dust off your imagination and jump on the tram. The tour is beginning.

Photo by Charles J. Alsheimer

Chapter II

Getting Started...
Make a Commitment,
Develop a Plan

Imagine the NorthCountry tram pulling into a small food plot. You get off and walk until you're standing by a tired old apple tree. Its top branches are severely pruned, and its limbs droop under the weight of bite-size apples. Deer tracks and droppings litter the ground. You notice a buck rub and scrape a few yards away. Hanging from one branch is a frayed yellow nylon rope.

Twelve years before, this tree had laid on the ground, the victim of a spring ice storm. The rope had been used to haul, hoist and secure the tree into an upright position.

This tree and its rope are symbols of our commitment to creating quality wildlife habitat. Most people would have left the tree on its side. For us, raising it was a symbolic act. Two weeks earlier, we had "released" the stressed apple tree from the grips of crowding brush, competing trees and a dense overstory. The work we did that day with a chainsaw was exhausting but rewarding. We saved the apple tree from a slow, certain death. It hadn't borne fruit in years, but we went to sleep that night dreaming of deer feasting on its future bounty.

Can you locate the deer in this photo? Thick cover like this provides food and cover for whitetails. Creating dense cover is relatively easy as long as "stemmy" material or wooded areas already exist. If you are working primarily with open spaces like fields, planting is the answer, but it takes more time and money.

That had been our first habitat project, so we were crestfallen when we visited the property after the ice storm and saw the apple tree on its side. Righting toppled trees is not a practice we recommend, but on that early-spring day, the job needed to be done. After all, we had committed ourselves to creating quality wildlife habitat. Turning this tree into an apple-producing food source was part of our plan. We were determined to succeed.

Make a Commitment

Quality habitat development requires a landowner to commit time and money. How much? That depends. Some properties

Getting Started... Make a Commitment, Make a Plan

require more time and others require more money. At a minimum, you'll need basic tools such as chainsaws and pruning shears. More likely, you'll also need food-plot implements such as tractors, plows, disks and ATVs. Further, high-quality seed is a must, as is lime and fertilizer. Oh yes, you'll also need knowledge, but that's why you're reading this book.

Most habitat enthusiasts are do-it-yourselfers. In fact, many are weekend warriors with no more than a dozen workdays per year to spend on habitat projects. But a great deal of the satisfaction in deer hunting — and the creation of quality habitat — is doing the work yourself, or at least planning and organizing the work for others. Nothing is more satisfying than seeing a half-dozen quality animals using a food plot you cleared and planted yourself. We did most of the work on the Demo Center, and we would not trade

Creating food plots is part of most habitat-development programs. Food plots planted in high-quality BioLogic forages create tons of highly nutritious forage for whitetails. This 1-acre food plot will be used by a dozen or so deer each day and even more each night.

the thousands of hours we spent together for anything. Doing the work yourself and with friends or relatives brings you closer to the land and the people you care about.

Habitat development does not happen overnight. The work you do today might not benefit wildlife for months or even years. Yet we are confident every practice in this book will benefit

•••••••••••••••••••••••••••••••••••••
Are you a quick-fix person? If so, habitat development might not be for you. But if you're patient and want to be a good steward of the land — and you enjoy hunting and viewing quality animals — you will likely get hooked on habitat development and quality deer hunting.
•••••••••••••••••••••••••••••••••••••

wildlife, if implemented correctly. Are you a quick-fix person? If so, habitat development might not be for you. But if you're patient and want to be a good steward of the land — and you enjoy hunting and viewing quality game animals — you will likely get hooked on habitat development and what we call "quality deer hunting." Once that hook is set, few of us escape. Habitat development is contagious and self-perpetuating.

Let's discuss how to get started.

Finding Land to Buy

First, you need land with which to work. The most attractive option is to own the property where you'll be working. Ownership eliminates the hassles of landlords, lease arrangements, gaining and maintaining access, and so on. It allows you to do what you

Getting Started... Make a Commitment, Make a Plan

want with your land, and when you want to do it. The most common question asked in Neil's seminars is this: "How many acres do you need to work with to improve hunting through habitat development?" His answer: "How many do you have?" We believe you can always improve your hunting through habitat development. You might not be able to manage a big herd (most experts say about 1,000 acres is required to truly manage deer), but you can change things for the better. Most landowners we work with own between 60 and 600 acres.

Of course, ownership is expensive, with good hunting land usually starting at $1,000 per acre. Not only that, but good property is difficult to find. NorthCountry Whitetails handpicks and brokers deer hunting properties. Our waiting list far exceeds the properties available. Although land prices might appear prohibitive, it helps to be creative when considering a purchase. Recreational property often contains valuable timber that could — and often should — be cut to offset the land-purchase price.

In addition, many landowners are willing to "hold the mortgage" on a property, because bank financing for undeveloped land can be difficult to obtain. After all, banks often ask for a down-payment of 20 percent or more of the purchase price. You can often do much better with an existing landowner who is eager to get out from under the tax burden.

You should also explore state and federal programs such as land set-asides when you shop for land. These programs often cut monthly land payments in half. In fact, deeding a property to a state or pro-hunting conservation group, while retaining perpetual use of the land for specified purposes, might allow you to obtain a property for free or nearly free. In such cases, you buy land and then sell it to an organization, but you retain specific usage rights. We have seen highly creative deals done this way.

Bottom line: Owning land is the best way to go, but it requires money. Creative financing is often the way to obtain exceptional properties with little or no cash. Even so, it's not easy. But if you can pull it off, you just might have paid yourself $500 or $1,000 per hour in land-use benefits.

Be wary of group purchases. Best friends today are often sworn enemies tomorrow, especially when money is involved. Try to purchase property alone or with as few people as possible.

•••
If you lease property, be sure to have a legal agreement with a stipulated length and strong renewal language. This ensures work you do today benefits others tomorrow.
•••

Hunting camps are notorious for breaking up because of financial disputes, especially when second- and third-generation owners are involved.

Leasing: A Good Second Choice

Most hunters wrongly believe they must own land to develop its habitat. Ownership is ideal, but not mandatory. Leasing is a realistic option. More and more property owners are interested in offsetting costs by granting access to hunters for a fee, and they're willing to allow those leasing property to do habitat projects.

Lease costs vary, depending on the geographic area and the lease's quality. In our area of Steuben County, New York, leases could be had for as little as $3 to $5 per acre in 2002. Other areas can cost as much as $20 per acre or more.

Getting Started... Make a Commitment, Make a Plan

If you lease property, be sure to have a legal agreement with a stipulated length and strong renewal language. This ensures the work you do today benefits others tomorrow. Although it's best to have your lease drawn up by a lawyer, be sure it's written in easy-to-read language. "Lawyer-speak" can spook the landowner and dash all hopes of an agreement. It's also wise to ask your lawyer to include an "option-to-buy" and/or a "first-right-of-refusal" clause in the contract. By doing so, you won't be helpless if the landowner decides to sell the land you've been working on and investing in. In fact, a first-right-of-refusal clause usually prevents a property from going on the market, keeping all sales conversations between you and the landowner.

Hunting By Permission: Be Careful

Another option, although not nearly as attractive as owning or leasing, is hunting by permission. "Permission hunting" is fading fast as private properties are tied up in leases. However, some landowners might grant verbal permission to hunt and perform habitat-management work. The key to the "permission-granted" option, once again, is securing access for extended time periods before investing time and money in a property. Try to be sure the friendly landowners will be there for the long run. You do not want to invest time and money in food plots and other projects, and then lose access privileges in the future.

Our 500 acres at the NorthCountry Habitat Demo center started as a 150-acre acquisition. Next, we added a lease of 250 acres. Five years later we converted the lease into a purchase because of the option-to-buy clause in our lease. We completed our third purchase, of 100 acres, soon after. Acquiring hunting property in a piecemeal fashion is not unusual. Seldom do you find one piece of ground that is ideal for all purposes. Most hunters want

Good farmer/hunter relations often result in permission to hunt. But be careful. Access permission is often a temporary condition, and it is difficult to manage habitat with only a "permission-to-hunt" agreement. Leases are far better. Land ownership is better yet.

or need more. Typically, hunting landowners start with one tract and add others as opportunity and money allow.

Start with a Site Evaluation

Once you have secured property to work with, it's time to develop a plan. Begin with a site evaluation, which is best conducted by a habitat-development specialist, especially if you're inexperienced. NorthCountry Whitetails conducts dozens of site

Getting Started... Make a Commitment, Make a Plan

evaluations each year. We make recommendations depending on the client's goals and objectives for their property.

The Buckleys did our evaluation years ago. They visited the property and walked the entire acreage, examining its food sources, cover, access, security, boundaries and topography. They drafted specific recommendations and helped answer our implementation questions. They saved us time and money, and contributed greatly to our success.

While expert help is nice, it's not always necessary. In fact, some people prefer a total do-it-yourself approach. This book will help you get started and save you serious time and money.

Let's review what to look for during a site evaluation. Existing food sources are a critical focus of any evaluation. Volumes have

A habitat-development professional will conduct a site evaluation and write a plan tailored to your goals, objectives and the site itself. Pros can save you time and money, but be active in the planning and implementation. The more a landowner stays involved with planning, the higher the success rate and deeper the satisfaction.

been written on the whitetail's preferred foods, so do some reading before you start evaluating your property's food sources. When evaluating food sources, look for signs of what whitetails are eating. Check brush and trees for nipped twigs, buds and leaves, and look for evidence of foraging such as nipped clover and grasses. Also look for potential food sources and possible food-plot sites. Does the property have abandoned fields or tillable acres? Look for opportunities to drop trees and create new browse by encouraging regeneration. We call this a "browse-cut." Look at soil content and soil quality, especially moisture availability. Today's brush-choked field can be tomorrow's clover plot. It might just require a weekend of work.

In evaluating a site, you must take stock of what the deer are eating and what they don't touch. At the same time, identify opportunities to create food sources through "intervention."

Evaluating Cover

Cover is just as important as food. In fact, if your property is surrounded by abundant food sources or is in farm country, cover might be more important than food sources. Look for dense, brushy, impenetrable thickets that deer love to frequent. Remember, the deer's world exists from ground level to a height of about 5 feet. Above that, with the exception of mast-producing trees, little else matters to deer.

Whitetails — especially big bucks — crave a secure place to hang out. Dense cover is highly attractive to deer. Again, look at the property's potential as well as what already exists. A stand of 4- to 6-inch maple poles will make the ground almost barren, because these trees produce dense shade and don't allow anything to grow below. Deer find little use in such stands. However, if you

Getting Started... Make a Commitment, Make a Plan

This apple tree has been heavily browsed. In fact, it's unlikely to survive. Even though deer are fond of apple trees, browsing this severe indicates a food shortage. If additional overpopulation evidence is found, deer numbers must be reduced or food sources increased.

spend a day or two with a chainsaw, you can convert an acre of pole timber into a productive browse-cut. Two or three years later, the same site can be a home for the most reclusive white-tailed buck, providing ample food and cover.

Creating cover is often the most important habitat-management practice you can employ. For example, Dave Reitano and Peter Crawford are NorthCountry clients who manage a 170-acre property in central New York's farm country. The property is long and narrow. About 30 percent of it is tillable, and another 30 percent is covered with hardwood pole timber. The rest of the property features overgrown apple orchards with no ground cover, the result of dense shade from vines and climbing rose bushes. Deer passed through the property frequently and did some night feeding, but seldom hung around during daylight. The owners wanted

This deer is enjoying the benefits cover, which includes food and protection from predators and weather. In evaluating a property's suitability for whitetails, be sure to think about its cover potential.

to develop the property's daytime holding capability. Creating cover was the key, along with planting high-quality forage. Therefore, a chainsaw crew spent a few weekends thinning the orchards' overstory. The "fresh" sunlight allowed dense ground cover to re-emerge. Meanwhile, a logging crew took care of the hardwood stand.

These areas were soon on their way to becoming secure holding cover. The owners then added a few strategically placed food plots to concentrate the deer on the property, thus completing a turnaround in hunting quality. Within two years, the property became a holding property instead of a pass-through property. Dave and Peter enjoy quality hunts regularly.

Getting Started... Make a Commitment, Make a Plan

Access is Important

Access is the third major factor in evaluating property, especially in areas with high hunting pressure. Hunting properties must be accessible in order to realize their recreational potential. A network of trails and roads is important for managing a property. Access roads allow equipment to be moved from place to place to work on projects.

The NorthCountry Demo Center took a huge step when we created a truck-friendly access road to connect both ends of the property. This road allowed commercial lime and fertilizer trucks to reach almost all of our food plots, cutting labor and material costs dramatically. This access road is bordered by high-quality clover, and is often used by deer, turkeys and bears. It produces

A network of access roads is important to a managed property. Roads and trails not only provide hunting access, but they enable you to move equipment in and out of areas needing attention. "Forever wild" is a nice concept to read about, but if you want quality habitat, you need a network of roads to get some work done.

miles of ultra-attractive edge environment. The bulldozer work required to construct the road was significant, and at times ugly, but the outcome was worth it.

Not all access roads need to accommodate heavy equipment. Others can be ATV trails that allow you to get in and out of your property with little disturbance to wildlife. The same holds true for walking trails, which are equally important. When evaluating a property, look closely at access. Whitetails adapt to human activity on access roads, and are seldom panicked when we happen along. They usually just scamper away as we approach. Restricting your movement to access roads allows access and won't push wildlife from your property.

Pay Attention to Trespassing

Unfortunately, unwanted access must also be considered, especially in populated areas. Trespassing is a fact of life and not all "visitors" are desirable. When evaluating a property for purchase or lease, pay attention to the neighborhood. You wouldn't buy a home in the middle of a high-crime neighborhood. The same holds true for hunting land. Learn how many neighbors border the property and who they are. If known poachers and troublemakers are abundant, perhaps you should look elsewhere. Outlaws can make life miserable. Also look at roads that intersect the property. If your 100-acre paradise is chopped up by two or three public roads, it could be a security nightmare. Always look for properties that discourage access by unwanted visitors.

If you already own a "high-maintenance" property, you have no choice but to deal with it. It's never too late to implement a no-trespassing policy. This requires that you prosecute trespassers and aggressively post your property against trespassing. When

Getting Started... Make a Commitment, Make a Plan

looking at property, it's easy to disregard the trespassing issue. Don't! Each year, Neil answers hundreds of questions about trespassing from people at his shows and seminars. Trespass problems are one of his hottest topics. The issue is real, and you must address it early in your planning.

You cannot manage a property without managing trespassing. Pay attention to this aspect of ownership when considering a property for lease or purchase. If you already own or lease hunting land, concentrate on eliminating all trespassing.

Write a Plan: Goals, Practices, Budgets and Timelines

After evaluating a property, it is important to establish goals for the land. This is an important step, and the help of a specialist pays huge dividends. Not all landowners have the same objectives. Some want to grow trophy deer while others prefer to see an abundance of wildlife. Many want both. Once you set your goals, you must develop a plan to achieve them. The plan should outline habitat-development activities, including time and cost in order of priority, and the ease of successful completion. Early in the development of our NorthCountry facility, we identified dozens of wild apple trees in stressed, overcrowded conditions, including the one at the beginning of this chapter. They were in decline and seemed destined to be firewood. It was important to "release" them, that is, remove competing trees and brush.

We also needed to prune them to reverse the decline. This was not only a useful and logical first step, but it was also financially feasible for a start-up operation. It required only a chainsaw, pruning shears, safety gear, and a few pounds of fertilizer. Best of all, we finished the work with a feeling of accomplishment and optimism. We saw tangible results immediately when deer browsed the pruned limbs, and soon after we saw strong regrowth during spring and summer. A ruffed grouse hatched a brood under a pile of pruned limbs.

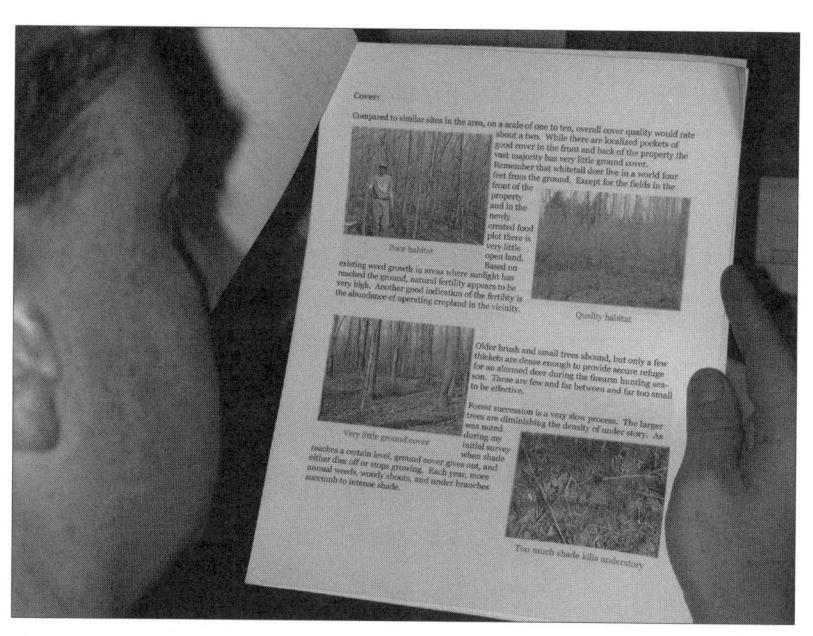

A plan developed by NorthCountry Whitetails typically divides the property into sections, and provides recommendations for each area. We also set goals and priorities, and recommend specific habitat practices to achieve them. We want landowners involved in the planning process. A sample plan can be found in the last chapter.

Getting Started... Make a Commitment, Make a Plan

Your plan should contain a clear statement of goals, a set of strategies to achieve the goals, a list of practices you intend to undertake, a realistic timeline, and an equally realistic budget in dollars and cents.

Set Priorities for Success

When identifying projects, be sure they are "do-able" within your time and expense boundaries. Nothing is more discouraging to beginning land-mangers than tackling a project that never ends or gets too expensive. Accomplishing a series of small projects is more rewarding and beneficial to wildlife than starting many and completing few, if any. Walk before you run. Take small steps and, if possible, work with a habitat-development specialist to avoid unnecessary mistakes that cost time and money.

Be sure to put your plan in writing, even if it's just an outline. Committing your goals and priorities to writing not only sharpens your thinking, but provides motivation. You don't have to cast your plan in concrete, but you'll find it helpful to commit it to writing.

This chapter is merely the bones of your plan. The rest of the book lays on the meat necessary to achieve quality deer hunting and habitat development.

Photo by Charles J. Alsheimer

Chapter III

A Chainsaw is a Deer's Best Friend

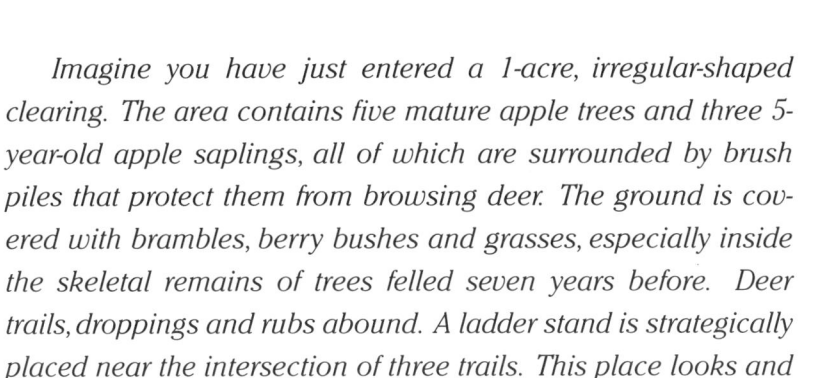

Imagine you have just entered a 1-acre, irregular-shaped clearing. The area contains five mature apple trees and three 5-year-old apple saplings, all of which are surrounded by brush piles that protect them from browsing deer. The ground is covered with brambles, berry bushes and grasses, especially inside the skeletal remains of trees felled seven years before. Deer trails, droppings and rubs abound. A ladder stand is strategically placed near the intersection of three trails. This place looks and feels like a deer hangout, but it was not always so. Eight years ago, it was canopied by sun-shielding pole timber. Nothing grew at deer level. There was no food and cover; just dirt and a few leaves strewn under the dense pole timber.

We call this place "Wayne's World," because it was the favorite hunting spot of our friend Wayne. Three decades earlier, this 20-acre section of sidehill was an eroding sheep pasture with a southern exposure. Fifteen years of successional growth resulted in dense brush, which gave way to a canopy of pole timber years later. A small stand of wind-deflecting pines

Does hang near cover for food and safety. This buck jumped this doe in thick cover. Does also use dense cover to hide from aggressive bucks. This doe has been driven into the open by the big guy.

bordered the clearing to the west. Overgrown apple trees and an occasional hardwood completed the habitat mosaic. For the first two to three years we owned our property, deer seemed to just hang out at Wayne's World. The hunting was super. But over time, we noticed the deer stopped frequenting this location. Even Wayne, who christened it his favorite place to hunt, began to hunt other locations. The hotspot grew cold, but why?

One afternoon in June, the answer came to us as we stood in Wayne's World. It was dark. Not night dark; just heavy, dense, canopied woods dark. A dense overstory of vegetation was thriving 20 to 30 feet above us, but nothing was growing on the ground. No wonder there were no deer. This was 2 o'clock in the afternoon, and no sunlight was reaching that critical zone of 5 feet and below. It was time — past time, in fact — to take action.

A Chainsaw is a Deer's Best Friend

The next winter, four men with chainsaws, an ax and a few wedges were again in the spot. In 16 hours of work, they created a relatively open half-acre of space, leaving only a few mature trees standing. They then piled the brush cuttings to strategically direct deer movements. We were on our way to restoring quality deer habitat to Wayne's World.

We cut it drastically, sawing all the poles to ground level. We planted a few apple trees to complement the old-timers, and stacked brush around them for protection from browsing deer, but other than that, we left the site alone. Today, briars and berry bushes grow everywhere. The apple trees are producing fruit, and deer sign is abundant. In just three short years, Wayne's World was once again a hotspot.

This scenario illustrates how the dynamic properties of nature are ever-changing, and can sneak up on you. Twelve years before, Wayne's World was a hotspot where deer hung out. Three years later, the same location

Browse is vital to deer and relatively easy to create. No matter how many crops are available, deer still need, and eat, lots of browse. A dense opening like this spot is a "bed-and-breakfast" stop for this big fellow.

Photo by Charles J. Alsheimer

was a dead zone for deer. The only deer we saw were on their way to other areas. Our chainsaw intervention transformed an area devoid of deer into a popular staging area and a favorite hunting spot.

Chainsaws Create Food

Motivated by the results at Wayne's World, we have since spent countless hours investigating the feeding habits of deer, and creating browse at the NorthCountry Demo Center. It's important to understand that most of a deer's food exists within four feet of the ground. Deer feed on forbs, leaves, grasses and browse stems. Hard masts like acorns are also a

Deer have browsed more than one inch from these shoots. This is not a good sign. It indicates a food shortage for deer in this area. You have two choices: create more food or reduce deer numbers. A combination of the two will probably work best.

A Chainsaw is a Deer's Best Friend

This twig is lightly browsed. Less than an inch from its tip has been eaten. The deer that nipped this twig got maximum nutrition for minimal effort. This is a sign that deer numbers and available food are likely in sync, assuming this is a preferred browse species.

favorite, as are soft masts like apples, lichens and mushrooms. The first 3 to 5 inches of new growth on a branch or twig provides the best browse. The average protein content of red maple browse on our facility is 5 percent to 6 percent. Most of the nutritious browse eaten by deer is in the last inch. After that, it becomes more difficult to digest as the deer chews its way down the stem.

When limbs within reach of deer are repeatedly browsed off, trees shift their growth energy elsewhere, and the new growth sprouts above the deer's reach. The food source disappears or worse, dies. To see this condition in the extreme, examine woodlots where livestock have fed. Virtually nothing is left at ground level. When you see conditions like this in the woods, you have real herd management problems: too many deer, too little food. Natural regenerating brambles and young tree stems are all very good food sources, but they grow at ground level and require lots of sunlight to prosper. Sunlight is the key, but an overabundance of deer can eliminate browse in even the sunniest areas.

We recently undertook a study with Charlie Alsheimer in which he placed cuttings from assorted browse species into one of his deer-research enclosures. We were interested not

Browse Species in Order of Preference
Percentages represent crude protein and crude fiber, respectively.

Species	May 15, 2001	Aug. 15, 2001	Dec. 15, 2001
1. Wild Apple	3.8% - 5.6%	11.7% - 12.3%	4.2% - 19.7%
2. Basswood	4.3% - 6.1%	6.9% - 7.4%	3.4% - 20.2%
3. Ash	4.8% - 6.7%	6.7% - 11.4%	3.3% - 30.7%
4. Aspen	9.1% - 12.9%	6.1% - 9.3%	5.1% - 17.6%
5. Hard Maple	7.0% - 8.8%	4.8% - 9.8%	4.6% - 25.7%
6. Red Oak	5.6% - 7.5%	6.8% - 11.3%	3.0% - 31.7%
7. Staghorn Sumac	4.1% - 6.3%	4.0% - 7.5%	6.0% - 28.0%
8. Raspberry plants	5.0% - 5.4%	N/A	N/A
9. Black Cherry	12.8% -13.4%	5.9% - 7.1%	3.2% - 18.2%
10. Wild Strawberry	3.1% - 4.1%	N/A	N/A

Non-preferred Species - Eaten if Other Browse is Unavailable

| 11. American Beech | 7.4% - 12.7% | 7.8% - 13.2% | 4.3% - 23.6% |
| 12. Striped Maple | 8.6% - 9.8% | 2.5% - 3.5% | 2.4% - 20.4% |

Highly Preferred Winter Food*

| 1. White Cedar | N/A | N/A | 4.2% - 12.7% |
| 2. Hemlock | N/A | N/A | 3.6% - 11.2% |

* White cedar and hemlock are highly preferred by Charlie Alsheimer's enclosure deer and by wild deer during winter. Their preference for these two browse types at this time of year rivals their preference for the top four preferred foods on the above list. However, white cedar and hemlock are not browsed much, if at all, the rest of the year. *(Protein data was determined by the NEAS Diagnostic Laboratory of Cornell University.)*

Table 1

only in what the deer preferred to browse, but the protein content of each browse species. Charlie documented the browse in order of the deer's preference from greatest to least, but when the protein results came back from the NEAS Diagnostic Laboratory of Cornell University, we were surprised. The deer did not consistently gravitate to high-protein food, as has been frequently stated in print. Their preferences changed with the time of year. The results are found in Table 1.

Because Charlie is familiar with the deer in this study, he could also note individual preferences. Deer, like humans, seem to prefer certain foods. For instance, one of Charlie's bucks loves to eat American beech browse, while the other deer in the enclosure seldom, if ever, browse beech. Charlie also has a doe that loves aspen and always chooses it over other foods.

A lot can be learned about deer from observing their feeding behavior, and an astute observer can learn a lot about his property by analyzing those feeding behaviors, especially if he observes it year-round. You don't need to be an expert to observe which food sources deer use on your property. Don't be surprised if they don't fall in line with what the experts report.

Therefore, don't accept everything you read about deer behavior as absolute truth. Sharp eyes and an inquisitive mind reveal much. Always, always observe and analyze the wildlife — especially deer — on your property.

Browse as a Population Index

Evaluating browse use helps estimate the amount of deer food available in an area. Look at a plant and see if the 1-inch tips are browsed off, or if 3 or 4 inches of the stem or twig are torn away. The entire stem might be consumed by deer during a severe winter. If you find gross consumption, your deer need more and better food sources. Increasing the amount of deer browse helps correct the problem. When you produce enough browse tonnage, and other nourishment such as food plots, your deer will begin to use just the ends of the stems. This is progress, but you need to get to where they eat only the last inch or half-inch.

Reducing the number of deer on your property is another strategy to keep a constant supply of quality deer browse available. Many wooded areas have so many deer that they all but eliminate forest regeneration. This is a bad situation for the deer and woods alike.

White-tailed deer, and most wildlife, for that matter, thrive in a thick environment. Now that Wayne's World has been restored to excellent deer habitat, guests on our tours see the contrast with an adjoining woodlot, which we left uncut for demonstration purposes. At "deer level" you see a dense stand of maple pole timber up to 12 inches in diameter, and nothing else. The crowns have grown together, preventing most of the sunlight from reaching the forest floor. Little food or cover is available. This is prime "people habitat," but deer do not spend time in this wide-open woodlot. They prefer the thick ground cover of Wayne's World.

A Chainsaw is a Deer's Best Friend

This aggressive clearcut at our facility covers about 5 acres and runs through the center of a beautiful stand of oaks. In two to three years it will be "prime real estate," providing a travel corridor throughout the woods as well as a "bed and breakfast" among the relatively open oak timber. Talk about structure!

Chainsaws Create Cover

Wildlife habitat should be thick enough to make it difficult for people to walk through, and almost impossible to sneak through. Brambles and underbrush hide deer and make noise when people move through, alerting deer to slip out the backside unseen. Concealing cover can be anything from timbered treetops or underbrush near a small rise or ridge, to a dense stand of pines or spruce. A quick escape route helps deer feel comfortable in these areas. The more cover the better. Deer prefer to stay within 60 yards of dense cover so they can disappear in two to three seconds.

Deer, like fish; are drawn to structure. The fish structure analogy is helpful when thinking about deer. If you have a

Photo by Charles J. Alsheimer

This buck is secure in this dense cover. His food is within steps of his bed. It is impossible for a hunter to approach quietly, so he can disappear long before a noisy human can get within his danger zone. This is quality deer habitat!

wide-open, one-dimensional forest or woodlot, you must drop trees and create structure. Plants will grow where daylight reaches the ground, producing different levels of growth and cover. Another fish analogy is that big fish prefer structure, in part, because it attracts smaller fish (food and bait). Deer also need cover and food, so they are attracted to structure in their habitat. In the case of big bucks, the does that frequent the structure are bait. When creating structure, first consider areas around natural or existing food sources, such as apple trees or clusters of oaks. Structure in conjunction with food is a tough combination to beat.

Try to create little pockets of cover 50 to 60 yards across throughout your property. These areas of structure will attract

A Chainsaw is a Deer's Best Friend

does, creating the prime environment for hunting bucks. During the pre-rut and rut, bucks will go from structure to structure searching for that doe in heat. The goal in these small cuts, which cover up to 1 or 2 acres, is to maximize food diversity and create cover. The chainsaw is the tool of choice.

Plan Before You Cut

Chainsaw work can also help control deer movement. Strategically cutting and placing felled trees manipulates how deer travel through the property. The goal is to create predictable deer movements. Trees left on the ground can guide deer movements through certain locations, allowing you to

This timber has been leveled, leaving plenty of room for sunlight to reach the ground and "inspire" vegetation. Brush will be piled strategically to alter deer movements and protect young trees from being browsed. Dense spruce will also be planted in strategic areas. This area will be a deer hotspot for about the next 10 years.

beat the whitetail's nose and set up a high-percentage downwind ambush.

Aggressive cutting creates what we call "browse-cuts." These are akin to clearcuts, but because clearcuts have developed a bad name, we prefer to call them browse-cuts. Browse-cuts are also usually smaller than clearcuts, which got their bad name because they often cover hundreds of acres, and create large disturbances to the terrain.

It is difficult to remove too many trees in a browse-cut. More often than not, landowners are too conservative with the saw, and leave too many trees, which shade the ground after a year or two of growth. We drop almost all the trees in the cut, from 18 to 20 inches down to 2 inches in diameter. We convert mature trees into saw logs and sell them. We cut smaller pieces for firewood, but we always leave some in the woods, especially treetops. It might be more important to get structure into the area than to harvest every stick of firewood. Leaving treetops in the cutting area is the quickest way to create ground structure. Try not to leave tops more than 4 feet in the air. That way, deer can browse the tender tips, especially if you are sawing in winter, which is the preferred time to cut. Tops kept close to the ground will also create a better-looking woodlot.

Create Living Brush Piles

We create living brush piles by dropping small trees or shrubs without cutting them clear through. We do this by felling small trees with a cut that doesn't sever it from the stump. The tree will lie on the ground and remain alive for perhaps a few years, providing thick cover and nutritious browse. Shrubs and small trees in the 3- to 6-inch range respond better to this treatment than do large ones. This maximizes the amount of food tonnage, and provides cover for other wildlife. You can also push over small trees with a bulldozer or tractor to create living brush piles. These will live even longer.

Leave Tree Tops on the Ground

The work done in Wayne's World is an excellent example of a browse-cut. This area was enhanced by planting several young apple trees and "releasing" several old and overgrown ones. We "released" them by removing the overstory and surrounding brush that competed for moisture and soil nutrients, and then pruned their spindly limbs, and fertilized the root system to increase apple production. We protected the young

This tipped-over tree will live on its side for a few years, providing dense cover and food for deer. For a living brush pile, push pole timber over with a tractor bucket or bulldozer, or cut them most of the way through and let them settle to the ground.

plantings from becoming deer snacks by piling brush in a 6-foot diameter around the sapling, 2 or 3 feet high. These treetops produced a "cage" that prevented deer from eating the young "whip."

Tops on the ground provide a caging effect that allows native tree species to regenerate. Deer choose not to walk through the downed tree tops because of their density. This reduces browsing dramatically. The spaces between limbs become protected nurseries for re-emerging trees and shrubs.

Treetops can also be stacked densely to create habitat for all kinds of critters. Build your wildlife brush pile by putting the largest logs on the bottom and stacking brush to about 6 feet high. This setup attracts rabbits and other small game.

The most effective way to lay out a browse-cut and create structure is to make a series of quarter- to half-acre cuts in a wooded area, felling most of the trees. Drop all the trees into a few strategically chosen target areas, creating small, dense structures. The area under the tops will regenerate tree growth, while the unprotected area should produce knee-high ground growth around the outer fringe. Another approach is to cut long "power lines" through the woods, which will become browse and travel corridors.

Cut Strategically, but be Aggressive

Good wildlife habitat should look nasty. You might even be embarrassed to show people the cutting for a couple of years, because of its appearance, yet you will see progress. At the NorthCountry Demo Center, we show before and after browse-cut areas. This helps visitors gain the confidence to aggressively cut for browse and cover. Don't be alarmed when you create habitat. In addition to high-quality food plots, we want native species to regenerate, and this will occur only if you put light on the ground. At the Demo Center, we are constantly setting back Mother Nature's natural succession. Deer feel more secure in these environments.

Remember Wayne's story? The first time he walked in there after the browse-cut, he said: "What did you do? This place used to be beautiful." We created 1½ acres of brush piles and downed trees. It's important to know what a browse-cut looks like. If you only cut to where you are aesthetically comfortable, you probably aren't cutting enough. Today, Wayne's World once again looks beautiful, especially to the deer that hang out there.

This browse-cut is a "mess," but it's a beautiful mess from a deer's perspective. New shoots are already coming up, and by summer the place will be a mass of green. This area will be productive for about 15 years, and then out comes the chainsaw again.

Our most recent cuts have been ultra aggressive. It looks barren now, but in no time this browse-cut will provide whitetails everything they need to survive. Planting the center road in clover will be a bonus.

In hindsight, we should have been even more aggressive in cutting Wayne's World. We reached a point in our cutting and clearing where we believed we needed to leave some trees. Now they have grown, and they need to come down. The chainsaws must come out again. A successful browse-cut maximizes light. With trees 30 to 40 feet high, the entire food source is in the treetops. Plus, the trees' roots suck valuable nutrients from the soil that could be used by browse-generating plants. As soon as you drop those trees, you establish cover and browse for the next year. In fertile areas, browse will spring up almost immediately.

The first year, you can expect existing stumps to send up shoots, and you will see occasional forbs, grasses, brambles, blackberries and raspberries. The second year will show a dramatic increase in woody stems, brambles and stump shoots. Typically, brambles begin taking over in the third year, to be followed in later years by larger and more aggressive woody stem development. If you have an environment with poor soil, regeneration can be enhanced with a dose of lime and/or fertilizer. This can accelerate regeneration by a couple of years.

A Chainsaw is a Deer's Best Friend

Not only is the chainsaw a deer's best friend, it's a habitat manager's best friend, too. With an investment of about $500 for a quality saw, a pair of chaps, and a safety helmet with ear and eye protection, you can do wonders for wildlife, especially white-tailed deer. With a chainsaw, you can do years of habitat-development work without owning a tractor or building a food plot. It's usually the best way to begin improving your property.

Some habitat managers prefer herbicide treatments to the chainsaw. Called "hack and squirt", you simple choose the tree, hack it with an ax or other cutting tool, squirt the cut with an herbicide. The tree starts to die shortly thereafter. It is reported to be highly effective and much less labor intensive than a chainsaw. We prefer the instant gratification of seeing the tree on the ground as the tops provide browse and cover and we are better able to shape the clearing.

Photo by Charles J. Alsheimer

Chapter IV

Property Access: Preventing and Creating

The NorthCountry tram turns down an access lane, which leads from a seldom-used public dirt road to a beautiful 40-acre stand of oaks. You stop in front of a cable gate that separates the public road from the lane. Three well-used deer trails cross the road within sight. Deer are crossing the public road at will. Up drives a rundown pickup truck with three scraggly passengers staring out. They are riding the roads a month before deer season, looking for "hunting" opportunities.

Deer sign is everywhere, but road hunters won't stop here. Displayed prominently is a plywood-backed yellow aluminum sign stating, "POSTED AND PATROLLED." The sign is just one of dozens displayed along the public road. The sign sends a strong message to would-be trespassers. The gate, which secures this right-of-way, sends another strong message against trespassing: Someone is serious about security on this property, judging by the gates and signs. It was not always this way, however. Twelve years before, this oak flat was "free range," and hunters from all over the area came and went. Only a few scattered signs were posted, and the landowner lived in California. Now, only invited guests dare enter this property.

Property access is about two things: making access easy for legitimate users and denying it to everyone else. Both are vital to managing habitat and quality deer hunting, but the issue of denying access arises most often in conversations with landowners.

Get the "No Trespassing" Message Out Quickly

One week after we bought the NorthCountry property, we were huddled around a July campfire when a truck came up the dirt road. It pulled over and we met our neighbor Willis for the first time. "So, you're the new owners," he said. "Going to hunt?"

"Yes, we plan to hunt, and we'll post the property against trespassing," I said.

• •

Property access is about two things: making access easy for legitimate visitors and denying it to everyone else. Both are vital to managing habitat and quality deer hunting.

• •

"Good luck!" he said slowly. "This property has been open hunting for years, and a lot of people will still feel that way. They've always hunted here. People won't quit just because you say so. You'll have your hands full keeping them out. And if you try to ... Oh well, you'll see."

Absentee landowners often have this problem. In fact, immediately after acquiring new land, you can expect to face trespassing problems, even if you live on the property. They will be short-lived, however, if you take the proper steps.

Property Access - Preventing and Creating

This "bulletproof" gate sends a no-nonsense message to would-be trespassers. It says, "These people are serious about their privacy and will take measures to preserve it." Simpler gates can be bought at most feed-and-seed stores for about $50.

Soon after our conversation with Willis, we began a security program on our property. We took obvious, deliberate steps to send the message that hunting without permission would not be allowed. First, we posted the land. Next, we contacted the sheriff and game warden, told them who we were and what we planned to do. We said we were posting the land, and asked them to help spread the word. Before long, locals knew the rules had changed on the "old McChesney place."

It was important to send the signal that we were reasonable people, but we insisted on ground rules. We let the locals know we might still grant permission to hunt or trespass, but we needed to know who was there, and when and what they were doing. We insisted on a policy of hunting by written permission only. With

This cabled gate is covered with 3-inch PVC pipe. The white pipe is visible and less likely to cause accidents than hard-to-see steel cable. The posted sign in the middle adds the final touch. We used scrap material, but the new stuff costs less than $10.

this policy, you can be viewed as a good neighbor while gaining control of your property. It also allows you to meet many of the people who have already hunted your property. Then it's easy to sort out the "undesirables" from the "maybes." You can then begin to explain your hunting-management program, and tell them why it's not a good idea for them to hunt on your land. In other cases you might include them in "management-deer" only hunts on specific days. You can also meet "contacts" who might help with your program. In our experience, aggressive posting discourages all but the most obnoxious trespassers.

Property Access - Preventing and Creating

Gate All Public-Road Access Lanes

Next, we gated all of our access lanes with a visible signal of ownership and restriction. For our main gate we chose an impressive welded-pipe structure that signaled, "Serious owners live here." We shut off most of our access roads with a cable threaded through two 6-foot pieces of 3-inch white PVC pipe for increased visibility and safety.

This sign is an excellent example of how posting should be done. The sign is supported by a board backer. It has aggressive wording and it's highly visible. It costs about $2 per sign, but is well worth it in the long run.

Gating and posting access roads is a must if you're to manage your property. You can't afford to have trespassers running deer from your property or harvesting deer without your knowledge. But controlling your property is also crucial for liability reasons. Just thinking about the safety implications of trespassers sneaking around while you or friends are hunting should make you shudder. One accident could ruin a lifetime of hunting for you, your family and friends, and possibly destroy you financially.

Post Aggressively

Posting is usually done with some sort of signage. Signs are available in three types: paper, plastic or aluminum. States and municipalities have different laws, so check local regulations to ensure you post your property legally. It's no fun to have a trespasser beat you in court because of a technicality in posting regulations. But don't settle for the legal minimum when posting. You might have to post more aggressively than the law requires in order to be effective.

Paper signs are the least expensive, but require the most maintenance. You must walk the boundary and replace them every year. Plastic signs are much better, with most lasting about five years before fading, cracking and pulling out at the nails. Aluminum signs are the most durable, especially when paired with backer boards. This last option is more expensive, but wood-backed aluminum signs often stay on a tree 15 to 20 years. Custom-printed metal signs cost about $1 each. Pressure treated backer boards cost about 50 cents. In the long run, they're much more cost-effective.

The preferred method is to fasten the signs to boards before heading to the woods. Backer boards should be pressure-treated 3/8-inch plywood or 3/4-inch boards. Rough-sawn scrap boards are excellent, but the necessary 11-inch width is difficult to find. When posting, drive aluminum or galvanized nails through the board/sign and into the tree, leaving an inch of nail protruding to allow for tree growth. Center-fasten the backed signs with two or three nails.

The backer boards and metal signs send a signal that you're serious about restricting access. Put yourself in a would-be trespasser's shoes. He is driving down the road and sees aluminum

Property Access - Preventing and Creating

Tired old signs like this are an invitation to trespassers. Perhaps the landowner has moved, but certainly he does not care enough about trespassing to keep his boundaries well-posted. Paper signs quickly turn old and must be regularly replaced.

signs with backer boards, clearly visible and closely spaced. Then he enters a stretch of road with old signs that are beat up and erratically spaced, perhaps hanging by one nail and difficult to see. If you were him, which property would you avoid and which would you poach on?

As a general guide, make sure potential trespassers cannot cross a property boundary without seeing a sign. In thick areas, you might place one every 30 yards, but you might get by spacing them 70 yards apart in more open areas. Also, post signs often near pullovers on roads and in human travel corridors such as draws, ridgetops and clearings. You can usually predict where a human will try to cross your line.

Certain states require that signs comply with legal specifications. Usually, signs must be of a certain size and include the landowner's name and a clear message against trespassing. When the law allows, include words of your own that send the strongest signal possible, such as "Patrolled, Prosecuted." If legal, include the law's maximum trespassing fine. In our area, the maximum fine for trespassing is $250. This is spelled out in black and yellow on every sign we post. Even though judges often slap trespasser's hands with a warning or a token $50 fine, stating the maximum penalty makes trespassers think twice.

• •

If legal, include the maximum trespassing fine on your signs. The law in our area sets the maximum fine at $250.

• •

Carry one of your signs into court to show the judge what the trespasser ignored. This helps you get the maximum fine imposed on trespassers. It has worked for us several times.

Yellow signs are the most visible. White signs don't show well in snow. If you have property along public roads, keep your signs visible by mowing roadsides and trimming around sign trees.

Don't skip open spaces just because you don't have a tree to hammer a sign onto. Fields and open spaces require metal or rot-resistant wooden posts. Another option might be utility poles, but check with the company that owns them before fastening posters to them.

The key is to do this job right the first time. Your entire effort must demonstrate a basic fact: If you're serious enough to maintain your boundaries, you're serious enough to prosecute anyone who trespasses.

Property Access - Preventing and Creating

This landowner is tough on trespassers. He not only posts his property, but surrounds it with one strand of wire fencing and a 20-foot-wide patrol road. There is no "accidental" trespassing here.

"Not on My Land, You Don't"

If you don't think posting signs is enough to discourage trespassers, run a strand of wire along your boundary. Better yet, put up a fence. A poster in the trespasser's face and wire behind it is difficult to ignore.

Also signal your presence by laying down fresh tracks on an access road or patrol road. This sends the message that someone is around and nobody better try anything. One of the first things we do on a hunting weekend is lay down fresh tracks in the mud or snow around our boundaries to intimidate would-be trespassers. This might sound extreme, but it helps to be proactive.

Hire A Person to Patrol for You

If you're uncomfortable encountering trespassers, hire someone to do it for you. Go to a law-enforcement officer and explain your needs. Ask for recommendations on how to hire a security person. They probably know one or more deputies who would help in exchange for pay, hunting privileges or both. This is especially true if you're managing for quality deer. We hired a sheriff the first three years during gun season, and he had everyone who came near the place looking over their shoulders. The sheriff patrolled the woods and spread the word in town. Every outlaw knew to go elsewhere. We still use hired security on our property, because it is impossible to be there every day of the hunting season. It's one more no-nonsense way to show we're serious about stopping trespassers.

When dealing with trespassers, firmly but politely ask for identification. Write down the pertinent information, as well as a description of the trespasser. Then ask them to leave your property. Avoid confrontation at all costs. Leave that to the law.

Property Access - Preventing and Creating

Prosecuting Trespassers is a Must

No one wants uninvited trespassing, yet many landowners are reluctant to enforce the laws. We confronted trespassers the first year we owned our property, just as Willis had warned us. Although we heavily posted the property, we encountered several trespassers on opening week of gun season. Being an absentee landowner and wanting to appear reasonable, we granted them one warning. We took down their names and license information, and told them this was their one "get-out-of-jail-free card." We told them if we encountered them again we would prosecute. This approach worked well for all but a few of the trespassers. All such encounters should be kept nonconfrontational. It is important to stay cool but firm. Both parties are carrying weapons, and an encounter in the woods could get out of hand.

Here's what we recommend: During the first encounter, explain your program, your expenses, etc., and that no one enters the property without permission. Then ask the trespasser to leave. Chances are he will ask to finish the hunt. Do not give in, and do not grant permission to stay the rest of the day. If you show any willingness, games will start. Tell him you and your friends are hunting, and you don't want to create a dangerous situation for anyone, including the trespassers.

Also, do not grant permission to hunt later in the season. Make it clear the next time they're found on the property they will be arrested. We have had a few repeat offenders, as will you, too. During our second year of enforcement, we had two individuals who didn't heed the first warning and came back the next year. The conversation was short and not too sweet: "Sorry to see you again, Bub. We told you last year we would prosecute you and now you leave us no choice." Again, we took back-tag information and told the hunter to leave. The conservation officer wrote them up later that week and we pressed charges.

In states where back-tags are not required, ask for identification. Write everything down, as well as a description of the trespassers. Many chronic violators hunt with phony ID's and licenses, because they have already lost their hunting license. If the person refuses to divulge anything, remember as many details as possible, including the type of gun or bow he was using. Find his vehicle and get its license number. A license is easily traced

• •
Fines will solve 99 percent of trespassing problems. We know of countless cases where trespassing is common simply because trespassers don't take the landowner seriously. Without prosecution, trespassing becomes a game.
• •

by authorities. Don't be a detective or a hero. Once you get the identification, simply contact a sheriff or conservation officer and report the violation. Let the law work.

If you say you're going to prosecute, you must do so. If you don't, trespassers will call your bluff and not take you seriously, and neither will law-enforcement officers. Sheriffs and game wardens are not social workers and they do not like "counseling" trespassers. They shouldn't have to spend their time issuing warnings. Asking them to have a little talk with a repeat trespasser is usually a waste of their time and yours.

If you call them, be prepared to prosecute. Your willingness to prosecute tells law-enforcement officials you won't waste their

Property Access - Preventing and Creating

When strangers are good enough to ask permission to hunt, provide them with a courteous, reasonable explanation if you're inclined to say no. You might work with this person in the future as you undertake your management program or hire security personnel. Reasonable people accept, "Sorry, but I can't." They'll still be friends in the future. Jerks are another matter all together.

time. More importantly, it sends shock waves through the community. News travels fast, telling everyone you mean what you say. A couple of fines will solve 99 percent of trespassing problems. We know of countless cases where people warn trespassers, yet the trespassers don't take them seriously.

Without prosecution, it becomes a game. The violator is having fun, and your deer management is nonexistent. The deer you're trying to grow are shot or chased off your land. Worse, you and your guests are put in danger, not knowing the whereabouts of every hunter on your property.

This officer is too busy to be called out to your property just to issue warnings. If the officer recommends an arrest, do your part and follow through with a complaint.

Denying Permission Requires Tact ... Usually

When encountering a trespasser, it's easy to get angry and lose your cool. Trespassers use up valuable hunting time, steal game and endanger everyone. But you must remain calm and in control. Use firm but convincing language. We point out that they created a dangerous situation for us, our guests and themselves. We tell them we don't tolerate it.

What do you do when politely approached by a solid citizen? Be a good neighbor. This is where tact and good responses are important, especially if the one seeking permission is a neighbor. If you're an absentee landowner, it's even more important to get along with the locals. The answer will usually be "no," but the challenge is to deliver it in a manner that shows you're an OK guy who just isn't in a position to allow others to hunt your property.

Property Access - Preventing and Creating

In short, how do you get neighbors to play by your rules? For those who ask permission, you should politely decline and perhaps offer an explanation. We've had success with this explanation: "We're going to be hunting here with our friends and family. If you're hunting our property, where will we hunt? We don't have anywhere else to go." If the person presses the conversation, explain further: "We're doing a deer-management program and have deer sanctuaries that are off limits to everyone. We rest the property on specific days and only shoot certain deer. We can't allow others to hunt. It's all regulated. We have invested a lot of money in this property for hunting."

If the person is still not convinced, we try this one: "If you really have to hunt here, maybe we can work out a business agreement where you share expenses. For 50 percent of our expenses, maybe we can talk. We put thousands of dollars into this place each year, and some financial help might be welcomed." That usually sends them packing.

Some persist and persist and persist. A firm "No, and I do mean no," is about all you can do. As they walk away, remind them the property is patrolled and you prosecute trespassers.

Deer Cameras for Surveillance

Remember, too, that you can always use security cameras. The motion-sensitive cameras used for taking pictures of deer work great. Hide them at known "man crossings" or where revenge-vandalism occurs. More than one law breaker has been rounded up by a hidden camera.

Creating Access for Your Use

Enough said on denying access. Let's move onto a more pleasant topic: creating access to your property. Without access, it is virtually impossible to manage a property — especially if you plan to plant food plots and conduct habitat-development projects. It's very helpful to have a substantial travel route through your property to do food plots and other work.

You should be able to travel this road with pickup trucks and tractors pulling moderate-sized implements. One of your goals should be to develop a road network that follows your boundaries. A patrol road on a boundary doubles as an access road. Place these roads 10 to 15 yards inside the boundary, which keeps it within sight so you can check for trespassers. If the road runs directly on the boundary line, neighbors will walk it.

Ready access is important to meeting habitat-development goals. It's desirable to lay out a network of roads that create access to all of your project areas. A main road with spurs is effective. You don't want your main access road to cross food plots, browse-cuts or secret hunting spots, but the spurs should lead to them — or at least close to them. That way you can come and go with ease. If roads run too close to deer staging areas, driving to and from hunting spots might displace your deer at dawn and dark. Deer will figure out this pattern and associate it with hunting. They might even become nocturnal. Try to create access around those areas and leave deer undisturbed. Even then, go easy on using access roads during hunting season.

Create Adequate Access for Farm Equipment

As you plan projects, develop two types of access: hunting access and farming or working access. To do serious farming or

Property Access - Preventing and Creating

This bulk-lime truck spreads 12 tons of lime over five food plots in about 30 minutes. The same job took two back-breaking days with smaller equipment and bagged lime. Without good access roads, no lime can be spread with a bulk truck like this.

food-plot work, you need roads to transport equipment and implements. These should be about 15 feet wide to accommodate large implements, and fertilizer and lime trucks. It takes all weekend to lime and fertilize a few acres with small spreader equipment and 50-pound bags of pelleted lime — which is four times as costly as bulk lime. But it can be accomplished in less than 30 minutes and at a fraction of the cost when done by a commercial application truck.

BioLogic's pH Fertilizer saves both time and money when bulk applications are impossible. It is a combination of fertilizer and lime in pelleted form and costs much less than buying individual bags of lime and fertilizer.

Keep major access roads away from wet spots, because you will use them heavily during the wet season in spring. If you can't avoid wet areas, drain them or build up your road with rock or gravel. It's also important to note that summer stream crossings can be far different in late fall and early winter. Fordable streams can turn into raging torrents, which shut down a hunt before it starts. Build good bridges or, better yet, avoid water altogether as driving through water creates erosion and can be very tough on equipment

Create Secondary Roads and Trails for Hunting

In our experience, deer are not too alarmed by motorized traffic on regularly used routes. Establish a traffic pattern through the year to develop a sense of familiarity with the herd. It is important that they have human encounters in the off-season that are not

This ATV trail winds throughout the entire property. Such trails provide hunters with ready access, and deer become acclimated to the disruption. It's important to stay on the trail and not surprise deer by wandering around on foot.

associated with predation. We want deer to see our John Deere Gator and ATV all summer. We want them to encounter us on foot only in certain areas. They just slip out of the way and let us pass, and then go back to their business. We want them to exhibit the same behavior in autumn when we go to hunting locations.

If you plan to establish a pattern with deer and vehicles, don't stop, stare and gawk from your vehicles, because this alarms deer. Wave and keep driving. Take hunters to a stand with a known vehicle — a pickup truck or four-wheeler — and pick them up the same way.

Stay on Known Roads and Trails

Do everything possible not to surprise deer on your property. Surprise encounters with whitetails sends them running, and spooked deer can run a long way. A hunter on foot is much more alarming than a recognized vehicle using a regular route. When we conduct the first tours of the year at the Demo Center, we surprise some deer. Later, we don't see any. They learn to pattern our tour. They hang back or stay bedded until we pass through. Never get off a vehicle and shoot or pursue game, even if it's legal. This can undo your patterning in a hurry. If you don't believe us, spend some time around deer that have been "hunted" from motorized vehicles. Chances are, you'll seldom see a deer.

Access is important to managing a property. Legitimate access facilitates management and makes hunting easier and more fun. Illegal access is a major problem and aggressive steps must be taken to eliminate it. Both require planning and action. Give it plenty of thought and do it right the first time.

Photo by Charles J. Alsheimer

Chapter V

Logging Roads & Clearings

The tram crawls down an old logging road that has been transformed into a smorgasbord of food for white-tailed deer. The road's 12-foot wide center is ankle deep in lush clover and chicory. Stump shoots, brambles, berries, forbs and other browse species grow 15 yards on both sides of the road. An occasional brush pile provides a home to ground critters, while old snag trees, ravished by woodpeckers, are homes to cavity-nesting birds. It was not always this way. Eight years before, this road was canopied, barely passable, and devoid of deer food. It was typical of most woodland roads. It was well on its way to becoming one with the surrounding woods, and years beyond producing usable food or cover.

In wooded areas, property owners often lack open space to plant or create deer forage. However, logging roads and clearings — created by a variety of disturbances — can usually be found in most wooded areas where other open space is scarce. They might be brushy and cluttered with new growth, but they can usually be cleared. These areas are priceless. They not only provide access, but they can also be converted to valuable feeding areas, capable of producing tons of nutritious forage.

This skidder is making a mess, but this logging road will be converted into a green ribbon of nutritious clover within three months. The main road will be planted, and the roadsides will be allowed to grow up in brush, creating a whitetail hotspot.

Developing Logging Roads and Clearings

Many logging roads and woodland clearings have good soil and moisture. Therefore, they can be planted with high-quality perennial seeds. Clover, in particular, makes an excellent logging-road forage. Planting logging roads is simple, but you must follow basic agricultural practices. That is, the soil must be fertile, moist and have a pH of around 6.5. Acidity is often high in woodlands, especially when oaks with their acidic leaves dominate the area. In most cases, roads near oaks and acid-producing conifers need lime applications. Planted areas also need a minimum of three to four hours of direct sunlight each day to ensure adequate growth, especially in spring and summer. If you have logging roads you want to plant, but not enough sunlight reaches the ground, eliminate some timber on the road's south side. The best logging roads

Logging Roads and Clearings

for planting in the North run north and south. This gives them direct sunlight from midmorning to mid-afternoon as the sun reaches its zenith.

Planted logging roads are especially valuable in summers when hot, drought-like conditions prevail. Because logging roads usually are found near shade-producing trees, they get a break from the scorching summer sun. The partial shade provided in summer keeps logging roads on our Demo Center in full production from June through August, long after our sun-baked food plots go dormant from heat and drought.

Most ATV equipment works well on logging roads. Be sure to buy high-quality equipment from companies like Plotmaster and Monroe Tufline. You don't want broken-down equipment ruining a weekend you set aside for planting food plots.

Planting Equipment

Logging roads can be worked with a variety of cultivating tools, from tractor-drawn disks to ATV equipment. Landowners who don't own farm equipment and tractors can do a decent job developing logging roads with an ATV and a Plot-Master. Monroe Tufline makes a heavy-duty line of ATV and small-tractor implements that are perfect for logging roads and clearings.

If you are doing a long stretch of road, we recommend an easy-to-transport spreader like this one from Monroe Tufline. This spreader is on its way from a food plot to a logging road. Hand-cranked "whirligig" seed spreaders are inexpensive, and work great for short-distance applications.

Logging roads allow you to generate forage in remote areas that cannot be reached with farming equipment. One of our NorthCountry clients has had great success developing woodland clearings and logging roads into feeding areas. First, he leveled and worked the logging roads with ATV implements. Two weeks later, he used Roundup® to kill the remaining weeds and seedlings. Because of soil conditions and the dense oak woods surrounding the roads, his soils are acidic and require lime.

Logging Roads and Clearings

He didn't have access to tractors or heavy equipment, but he could get into the area with a four-wheel-drive pickup truck. He took two trips to carry 2 tons of lime in the truck's bed, and backed it into a remote stretch of road. His son then drove slowly while he scattered the lime with hand tools. In 25 minutes, he shoveled enough lime to last several years. They also applied fertilizer with a hand-spreader. Using ATV implements, he roughed up the road and worked in the lime and fertilizer. The ATV's tires produced a firm seedbed by driving back and forth, a job his son relished. After they seeded the beds, he drove over it again to tamp the seed. Because of good moisture and adequate sunlight, the stands of Biologic Premium Perennial thrived. They were in their fourth year when we wrote this book.

As a result, our friend has a quarter-acre of knee-high quality forage tucked into the most remote part of his property. It is sur-

This logging-road planting is miles from the nearest public road, and rivals even the best food plots for quality forage. It is easily hunted and was planted in a half-day by its owner.

rounded by hardwoods and dense hemlock stands, and is set up perfectly for bowhunting. Deer craving a high-protein food source are regular visitors. This setup has produced dozens of deer for the freezer. Best of all, it is miles from a public road.

A logging road covered by lush clover looks like a green ribbon winding through the woods, and it produces more food than you might think. A typical logging road that's 15 feet wide — wider roads are even better — equals a half-acre every 500 yards. When planted correctly, this much road will grow up to 5 tons of quality forage each year. Plant another five or 10 half-acre roads, and you will add significant tonnage of top-shelf forage. An added bonus is that logging roads usually make better hunting setups than food plots.

Basic Plantings for Logging Roads

The proper method for planting logging roads is a simple step-by-step process. Basically, the technique is the same as planting food plots. First, determine the site's fertility with a soil test. Use a pH meter, which costs about $25, or take a soil sample to the farm-extension service or land-grant university for analysis, which costs $10 to $15. Be sure to indicate the forage varieties you intend to plant, and take your soil sample from several places at depths from 2 - 5 inches. Follow the soil analysis recommendations carefully. Liming and fertilizing will almost always be required to make plants grow better in woodland settings.

Next, use Roundup® or a similar herbicide to kill competing weed growth. After the Roundup® has done its job, it's time to cultivate, plow, disk or use hand tools to disturb the soil. Then, prepare a smooth, firm seedbed by rolling the soil with your ATV's tires or a lawn roller. You can drag almost anything behind the

Logging Roads and Clearings

This logging road would be improved if all trees within 15 yards of both sides were removed. That would allow sunlight to nurture clover that's planted in the road, and encourage brush to grow on both sides.

ATV to smooth and even the soil. For instance, an old bed spring works great, as does a 6-foot length of chain-link fence. Next, broadcast the seed with an ATV seeder or hand-crank seeder. Finally, press the seed into the ground with a roller or the ATV's tires to ensure soil contact. Make sure you do not bury the seed by disking or dragging. Seed buried deeper than an inch or so will die. Once nature adds the water, your plants should be up in a week or so.

Advanced Logging Road Development

A green ribbon of woodland forage is a great improvement to any property and a valuable addition to your habitat program, but a little more work will provide even more browse and four seasons of high-quality deer food. For the ultimate logging-road project, take it one step further to create a woodland smorgasbord. To do this, cut all trees 10 to 15 yards on both sides of the road, except for valuable timber and "hunting" trees. Leave the stumps and tops for cover and regeneration. Stumps produce shoots, and the tops provide security cover and allow browse to regenerate within the protective confines of their limbs. The suddenly abundant sunlight, along with adequate doses of lime and fertilizer, create an ideal environment and tons of food. Just imagine it: 15 feet of lush clover bordered on both sides by 30 or more yards of dense, high-quality browse winding through your woodlot. That's why we call woodland roads smorgasbords. In fall and winter, these places make ideal hunting spots, especially if you leave "hunting trees" along the roadways, and deer have a reason to use them year-round.

The doe at the end of this logging road is barely visible. The surrounding cover provides food and concealment. Deer travel these brush-lined logging roads heavily.

Our Demo Center has almost 50 miles of logging roads, many of which have been seeded and developed. However, not all log-

Logging Roads and Clearings

ging roads are suitable for high-quality seeds. When we develop a lengthy stretch of road, we apply the highest-grade seeds in the most choice, moist areas with the best soil. Biologic Clover Plus is ideal when you find good growing conditions on logging roads.

In dry, thin soils, we apply erosion mixes that consist of less expensive seeds. These sites will green up, but they might not turn into high-quality forage. Generic brands of clover, rye-grass and birdsfoot trefoil provide a good mix of forage in marginal conditions. At the least, the roads provide two bonuses: Deer use them to some degree, and the vegetation stops erosion.

The new growth along your roads also produces a privacy fence for deer, making them feel secure as you travel the road. If you often use the roads during the off-season and condition deer

Woodland openings create brush. Brush creates browse. Browse creates deer. This deer is eating the tips off twigs, where 90 percent of a twig's usable nutrition is found. Note the already-browsed twig above his left eye.

to your presence, you can sneak into your stands during the hunting season without alarming nearby deer.

Log Landings and Woodland Clearings

Every logging operation creates and uses some type of a cleared work area. Loggers call these sites landings or log decks. We call them miniature food plots. Like abandoned logging roads, they are usually covered with brush and young trees. But if they are less than 10 years old or even a bit older, they can be cleared in a day or so with hand tools, or in an hour or two with a bulldozer.

This small food plot was created on a log landing. These deer are secure in this out-of-the-way "mini-plot." In fact, whitetails seem to prefer such sites over large fields.

Logging Roads and Clearings

This buck is working the edge of a small woodland clearing. Bucks like him prefer to stay back from large open spaces. He didn't grow to this size by spending many daylight hours in the open.

These mini-plots are usually acidic because of sawdust and log bark left behind from the logging operation, but they can be converted into food-producing areas. Typically, log decks have shallow, compacted, infertile soil because of intensive work, but this can be fixed. Liming and fertilizing helps, as does roughing up the compacted soil. The right amount of lime allows more growth, and seeding with clovers when the ground is thawing in spring — known as "frost seeding" — helps knit bare spots together. In most cases, it's undesirable to plow and disk too much, because these areas have often lost most of their topsoil from the heavy-equipment traffic, and what remains is usually too compacted for optimum growing conditions.

Rather than repeatedly disturb marginal erosion-prone soils, it's often better to frost-seed a mixture of hard seed on the snow or frozen ground in early spring, and then control the weeds with selective herbicides. Note, when frost-seeding, expect germination rates of at least 30 percent of the seed, but not as much as with normal cultivation. The goal is to grow something green for deer, and to reach the point where natural seeding takes over. This allows you to get a food source established while gradually improving the soil's growing potential through mowing, or even by spreading topsoil or manure.

•••

Not everybody is blessed with open, tillable soils and areas that can be easily developed into food plots. Work with what you have wherever you find it. You will be amazed at the success you can achieve.

•••

Once you get the green stuff growing, don't redo it too often. Because log landings often have fragile soil, mow the area to add organic matter to improve soil quality. It might not perform like a high-quality food plot, but it will produce valuable forage for whitetails and can be improved over time. Manure adds to the soil production, as do leaves, hay bales or any other organic matter you find. Shred it with a rotary mower for rapid decomposition. Eventually, after you have rebuilt the soil's organic layer, you can establish high-quality perennials like BioLogic's Clover Plus.

Work with What You Have

Let's face it: Not every recreational property has several fields that can be used exclusively to grow high-quality deer forage. If your property has few open spaces, do what you can to create more openings and work with what you have. If you have the for-

Logging Roads and Clearings

tunate choice of developing a food plot or a logging road, put your money into the food plot. If you are not blessed with open, tillable soils and areas that can be developed into food plots, work with what you have, wherever you find it.

You will be amazed by the success you can achieve. The miles of logging roads on our Demo Center equal many acres of food plots. We haven't planted it all, because we prefer to develop tillable food plots in open space. Even so, we have planted more than half our roads in some type of green forage.

Best of all, the deer don't seem to know the difference, especially those huge, secretive bucks that survive by staying out of harm's way.

Photo by Charles J. Alsheimer

Chapter VI

Creating Sanctuaries

The NorthCountry tram is creeping through the center of the property. You begin seeing yellow signs to your left. The diamond-shaped signs are spaced more closely than you expect. And why are they here in the center of a property? The signs separate dense, impenetrable brush from more open terrain. The access road runs between. We can only guess what lies behind the sign, because humans have crossed the boundary marked by these signs only twice in the past 10 years. We know by trails and tracks that deer use this place heavily, especially during gun season, and sometimes we see them in the brush as we pass. We also see signs of huge bucks nearby. You're looking at one of several sanctuaries at the NorthCountry Demo Center. No one goes beyond these signs, but that was not always the case. Before the early 1990s, the sites were hunted heavily. Hunters put on deer drives through the area, and by the middle of gun season, deer could not be found in these parts.

If you want mature whitetails on your property, you must keep some areas off limits to humans. Actually, we create two kinds of sanctuaries: working sanctuaries and absolute off-limits sanctuaries. To appreciate the latter, let's follow a doe and her button-buck fawn.

Soon after buying our land, we lay out a 15-acre sanctuary. A year or two later, a doe finds this thick bedding area that humans avoid. She knows danger lurks on the property, but she feels safe there. So does her fawn. In fact, her fawn has never encountered a human in this secure area.

A year later in spring, her buck fawn leaves the property at the doe's urging, feeling the need to disperse. He leaves home and takes up residence two miles away. But, he remembers where safety lies, and eventually returns to the sanctuary when people pressure increases during hunting season. The doe goes back to

This doe will raise many fawns in this sanctuary during her life. Many of them will be bucks that might return to the site as mature deer when hunting pressure rises. One or two dispersing bucks might even stumble onto the sanctuary and take up permanent residence.

the sanctuary as well. The next season, as a 2½-year-old buck, he is again elsewhere, living and searching for does, but the opening of gun season brings a major influx of noise and human activity. The 2½-year-old buck remembers the haven and returns. He moves in and out of it, to and from food plots, but almost always at night.

Fast-forward four years. Our fawn is a trophy buck, and the urge

Sanctuaries should be clearly designated. This keeps guests from inadvertently entering the restricted area. Placing safe havens far away from property boundaries helps keep trespassers out. We use these specially designed aluminum signs.

to disperse has left him. He has become the dominant buck in the area, seldom straying far or long from this sanctuary. He might be nocturnal, but you know he's there because he leaves tracks and rubs as he comes and goes. Sooner or later, a doe will tempt him during her magical 24-hour period. He will lose all caution and run her into one of our hunting areas.

The sanctuary has created a quality hunting situation. We might see this monster only once or twice a season. A 4- or 5-year-old animal will knock our socks off. We know he is there and we're confident we will eventually see him. As long as we do not violate the sanctuary, the big buck continues to use it. Outside of

> *As long as you don't violate the sanctuary, a big buck will continue to use it. Outside of the sanctuary, you might encounter him on any hunt and maybe see him once per season. That's how we define quality deer hunting.*

the sanctuary, we might encounter him once per season. That's how we define quality deer hunting. The sanctuary has helped keep the high-quality buck on our 500-acre property, and given us a better chance of harvesting a trophy animal.

Locating Sanctuaries

Natural sanctuaries are often overlooked by hunters, but they occur everywhere. They can be nearly vertical sidehills, wide medians in a highway, weedlots behind the barn, or 1-acre overgrown building lots. Some 4- and 5-year-old bucks are out there, and that's where they hide during the season.

The good news is that you don't have to start hunting median strips on highways. You can hold quality deer on your property if you create a safe haven. Off-limits sanctuaries require complete protection. Don't risk visits by lost hunters or hikers. Paint the trees and hang signs. We created sanctuary signs to alert our hunters that they're about to enter a sanctuary. For a sanctuary to live up to its name, deer must have thick cover and food. Give the deer what they need, and they will stay.

Creating Sanctuaries

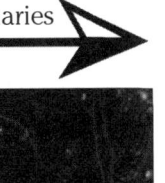

Neil shows off two consecutive years of antlers from this buck. The sheds were found within 500 yards of each other. The buck was killed on a food plot of BioLogic Clover Plus less than 100 yards from a "working sanctuary." The sanctuary was home to this big fella for at least three years, and probably more, because he was $6^{1}/_{2}$ when shot.

A working sanctuary is a site where we create habitat during the off-season. We enter these areas only at that time, typically during the winter. Even then, we enter them as little as possible, and cut trees to create cover and food. As the fawning season approaches, we avoid these areas completely, leaving them as deer havens. It remains that way through hunting season.

Entering a Sanctuary

If a wounded deer enters a sanctuary, we track it only at night. We go in with a lantern and no more than two individuals. Our entrance is low-key, with no shouting and loud talking. You'll never hear us yell, "Hey Joe, over here." By tracking only at night, we give deer a chance to sneak out under the cover of darkness.

Chances are, in fact, that they left the sanctuary as darkness descended, and you won't spook them at all. They can still return during darkness without risk of being killed by neighbors, and if you're lucky, they won't cut your tracks or know you violated their home. Avoid any daylight impact during autumn. Do not, under any circumstances, risk chasing deer from a sanctuary during daylight. It might be the end of the 5½-year-old buck you worked so hard to keep at home.

Sanctuaries do not have to be large. A 5-acre sanctuary is sufficient to hold a mature white-tailed buck. The thicker the sanctuary, the more animals it can hold. Its size also determines how many mature animals hole up there. For hunting, it's best to lay

Locating food plots close to sanctuaries increases the odds of catching a hungry buck outside of the site. It also concentrates does, which will lure him out during the rut.

Creating Sanctuaries →

Having entered a sanctuary, this buck will relax for the day. While in the sanctuary, he is in no danger from hunters. Although it's tempting to go in after him, it would be a huge mistake to do so.

out several small sanctuaries than one big centralized haven. That allows you to hunt travel corridors between the havens.

Try not to put sanctuaries near property boundaries because they're easily violated. People might wander in by mistake, take a shortcut, or walk past your posters in the dark. Sanctuaries lose their effectiveness even if violated once a year. One or two trips through the sanctuary can eliminate 10 years of off-limits discipline on your part. Mark it and mark it well. Make sure recreational and hunting guests know this rule is inflexible.

Have our sanctuaries worked? Year after year we see signs of huge bucks near these sites. We never know when a buck will walk out. Craig saw one particular buck just once two years ago, but he was an incredible animal, half-again as large as the 2½-year-old buck the big boy was harassing. Neil has also spotted a couple of sanctuary bucks, but they seem to come and go as ghosts.

Sanctuaries are easy habitat-development projects to design and complete. Once you locate it and mark it off-limits, you need do little more than avoid it. We also try to create and maintain a food plot or two near sanctuaries to entice a trophy buck to leave the haven for a bite, or to check out does that work the plots almost constantly.

• •
Sanctuaries are easy habitat projects to design and complete. Basically, once you locate it and mark it off-limits, you need do little more than avoid it.
• •

You can hunt the edges of the sanctuary with trees stands, or have a travel road around it. Deer learn they are safe and use it regularly as long as they are never surprised there or sense humans nearby are trying to kill them.

Sanctuary Size

How big should sanctuaries be? Well, a neighboring property of 300 acres has a 20-acre sanctuary laid out in a way that allows easy observation from a distance. Every year the owner, Randy, watches deer running to his sanctuary from high-pressure neighboring properties when the guns start going off. Randy said the deer get 30 to 40 yards inside, and then immediately relax, browse, bed or hang around 100 yards inside. They stay until early evening, and then head back out to feed. He is able to watch deer in his sanctuary and is certain they just unwind once inside its boundaries. We sometimes wonder if Randy spends more time observing deer in his sanctuary than hunting, but that is also what quality deer hunting is all about.

Our 500-acre property has two 15-acre off-limits sanctuaries. One is our original sanctuary, and the second became a sanctuary by default because there's no effective way to hunt it. We declared it off limits about six years after buying the land. When laying out a sanctuary, select places where the wind swirls, or where topography creates a difficult hunting situation. Such places make good sanctuaries, especially if they're dominated by dense, heavy cover. If you spook more deer than you see in a tough hunting area, why not let the deer have that area and restrict deer/human encounters to the outskirts? In addition to our two main sanctuaries, we also have several 1- to 2-acre havens we never enter and, of course, a half-dozen or so working sanctuaries.

We are especially cautious around our sanctuaries during gun season. We try not to encounter deer that are coming to and going from our sanctuaries during this time of vulnerability. We cut the bucks a lot of slack during the second half of gun season because, in our view, they've just about made it another year. Sometimes by the end of the season we're actually rooting for a particular buck to make it through so we might thrill at his tracks and rubs when the next bow season approaches.

A big part of quality deer hunting is the thrill of anticipation. Sanctuaries have a place in every quality deer hunting program.

Photo by Charles J. Alsheimer

Chapter VII

Woods Working — TSI

It's September, and the NorthCountry tram just entered a beautiful stand of hardwoods. The first of millions of acorns are beginning to fall in a 25-acre woodlot of red and white oaks. Virtually every oak in the woods is loaded with the whitetail's favorite mast crop. Looking up to assess the acorns, you see ample daylight penetrating the oaks' canopy. An occasional stump suggests a chainsaw has been working here. The woodlot and its wildlife are the better for it. Brushy cover obscures the ground.

This is a prime example of "timber stand improvement," or TSI for short. But seven years before, this was not the case. The oak canopy was overcrowded and intertwined. Acorn production was marginal, and virtually no food or cover could be found on the forest floor because sunlight was blocked out. With more than 50 percent of our property in hardwoods, we had to start working to improve our woodland habitat.

Deer get a great deal of their food from browsing, even when lush crops grow near browse sources. Woodlands are important

••••••••••••••••••••••••••••••••••
Deer get a great deal of their food from browsing, even when lush crops grow near browse sources. Woodlands are critical to whitetails and can dominate properties.
••••••••••••••••••••••••••••••••••

to whitetails and often dominate deer hunting properties. Improving your woodlands through TSI is a critical part of any management plan, and should be practiced by most landowners.

Timber Stand Improvement: Haircut for the Woods

In its simplest form, TSI is nothing more than a thinning haircut for your woodlot. Double- and triple-trunk trees usually are

Acorns are a preferred source of whitetail food. Deer heavily consume them in autumn. Timber stand improvement projects increase acorn production, and allow sunlight to reach the forest floor to stimulate new growth.

reduced to singles, and undesirable trees get cut to make room for quality trees. Foresters continually look up while marking trees for TSI. They want to thin the canopy enough so remaining trees have ample room to grow. They want to see blue sky surrounding the still-standing treetops when the thinning is finished. Selective thinning increases sunlight, creating a healthier stand of trees by accelerating the growth of existing timber and permitting ground-cover to regenerate.

Oaks also produce more acorns if they're thinned. In an uncrowded woodlot, valuable understory will be lush, providing browse and cover. TSI inspires a growth spurt for remaining trees, moving them closer to becoming mature saw-log timber, which can be turned into cash for additional habitat projects or land purchases.

People Habitat is Not Deer Habitat

Many of our Demo Center visitors "ooh and ahh" at a few unthinned red-pine stands we left untouched on our tour route. They look at neat rows of bare trunks and the carpet of brown needles and say, "Isn't that a nice area!" Well, it might be nice for a stroll or a summer picnic, but it's rel-

Symmetrical rows of tall red pines and a carpet of needles are great for summer picnics, but they do little for deer. This stand should be cut heavily. Exposing the ground to sunlight will produce prime cover in three to five years.

atively useless as whitetail habitat. Our friends the Buckleys call this "People Habitat." Don't confuse people habitat with deer habitat. The two habitats couldn't be much more different.

TSI is a time-honored, well-established forestry practice. With TSI, everybody wins, landowners and wildlife alike. Although TSI is a simple concept, it is best practiced with the assistance and guidance of a professional forester. A professional can mark your woodlot for thinning and leave the rest up to you, or he can arrange for a crew to come in and thin the marked stand for you. The forester will know which trees to keep and which to remove for the woodlot's long-term benefit.

When you thin trees, you can expect several positive outcomes. First, it allows remaining trees to accelerate their growth

This logger is cutting the poorer of two trees growing from the same bowl. The remaining, higher-quality oak will then grow faster, produce more mast, and become a more valuable saw log at harvest time. Daylight reaching the ground also creates valuable understory.

and add valuable board footage. A good working woodlot increases its value 7 percent per year, which isn't bad by most investment standards. Hardwoods like oak, cherry, maple and ash, to name a few, can generate major income. Softwoods like pine and spruce are also valuable. Besides increasing valuable board footage, TSI creates a healthier collection of trees in the woodlot. Trees left after thinning have adequate room for growth. Their canopies receive unrestricted sunlight, and their

> *Thinning woodlots allows valuable sunlight to reach the forest floor. This sunlight creates and stimulates the growth of underbrush, which provides food and cover for many species of wildlife, including deer.*

roots absorb more nutrients and moisture from the soil instead of sharing them with competing trees. Consequently, these trees are more disease-resistant and produce more mast.

Thinning woodlots allows valuable sunlight to reach the forest floor. This sunlight creates and stimulates the growth of underbrush, which provides food and cover for many species of wildlife, including deer. As a bonus, if you leave thinned treetops in the woods, they will be browsed the first year by deer, especially if the cutting is done in winter. The tops also provide shelter and cover for other animals, and protect new growth from over-browsing by deer. As we said, everybody wins.

Chainsaw Safety

A note on woods work: A chainsaw might be a deer's best friend, yet this tool can be very dangerous to man, especially weekend warriors new to chainsaws and strenuous work. In terms of chainsaw safety, it's wise to assume it's not a matter of if you will have an accident, but when. Anyone who runs a saw long enough will have some type of mishap. Take steps to protect yourself. The must-have pieces of safety gear include protective chaps and a hard-hat with an eye shield or goggles.

Hearing protection is also mandatory and will reduce fatigue. We deer managers often try to run a saw longer than we should, especially when we only get into the woods a day or two at a time. Fatigue sets in and we force the cutting and end up off balance. The saw can easily find its way to your thigh when your arms are weary. One wrong move and the chain can touch your leg, causing at the least a trip to the emergency room.

Besides a good chainsaw, you need the right protective gear. This professional cutter has eye, ear and head protection, plus cutting chaps, which will jam a saw before it gets to your leg. His cutting position is well balanced, with the saw away from his body.

Protective chaps will jam and stall the saw before it reaches your skin. Chaps have saved many loggers' legs. The helmet should have an eye

Woods Working — TSI

shield, and it should be used at all times. Wood chips fly everywhere when running a saw. Saws can also kick back and strike your chest or head.

That all sounds scary, but a larger danger looms overhead. Rotten or hung-up limbs often fall when you start to cut a tree. Loggers call these limbs "widow-makers" for good reason. Even a small limb can deliver a painful, crippling or fatal blow. You will never see it coming, so study what's overhead before starting a cut.

It's important to establish chainsaw rules and guidelines for yourself and friends. One good rule is never cut alone. Always work in tandem. It's also smart to take breaks every 15 minutes. Run the saw for short periods and then rest. Don't force the

Always cut with another person nearby. Not only is emergency help then at hand, but another person can keep you out of harm's way when saws bind or trees hang up. A partner also helps limit fatigue.

work when you're tired and don't cut with a dull saw. Dull chains tire you quickly and force you to cut off balance by leaning into the cut. It's also hard on the saw.

If you plan to do some cutting, attend a course to learn the proper techniques. It might save your life. Neil has cut into his chaps at least twice. Each time the saw bound up in the chaps' protective fibers before reaching his trousers.

We have also been clobbered by dead limbs more than once. When we conduct Demo Center tours, we point out where trees will drop and the consequences. Before cutting, study each tree to evaluate its danger. You must also study surrounding trees. Are dead limbs above you? Will they free-fall? Will the supporting branches move? Which direction will the tree fall? Watch leaners and hung-up trees. Depending on how they are stuck, they might be under enormous pressure, and virtually blow apart when cut. They could also bind your chainsaw's bar and force you to use another saw, or a wedge and ax, to get free.

Don't Forget the Fertilizer

Once the chainsaw work has been completed, some believe you gain great benefits by fertilizing trees. We use tree tablets designed to increase mast production. They're easier to use than loose fertilizer, and they supposedly increase acorn yield. Some believe fertilized acorns are more attractive to deer than run-of-the-mill acorns. We're not sure about all the claims, but we enjoy believing it helps.

These "wild" apple trees were rescued from a slow death 10 years before this photo was taken. We removed surrounding trees and brush, and pruned dead or stressed wood. These trees also get a dose of fertilizer each year.

Apple Trees Need Attention, Too

While we're on the subject of nurturing mast producers, a word about apple trees: The Demo Center has more than 40 "wild" apple trees scattered through its brush lots. When we bought the place in 1990, the seller said there was "one or two" of them. Each year we do some apple-tree work. Most of them were "released" the first 10 years we owned the place. We removed the overstory and cut back competing brush. Each year we also prune dead limbs and thin the interval limbs to make room for sunlight and encourage air movement.

We also fertilize them each spring by making dry-bar holes in the ground near the tree's drip line, and fill them with 5-10-15 fertilizer. We use a half-pound of fertilizer for every 4 inches of

Photo by Charles J. Alsheimer

This buck is enjoying the fruits of our labor. A little attention to apple trees every year or so helps produce good-looking fruit like this.

tree trunk. An easier approach is BioLogic's Tree-Paks. Each "tea bag" contains 1 ounce of fertilizer. Simply slit the ground with a shovel at the drip line and drop in the packs.

Most of our wild apple tress produce small apples each fall just in time for bow season. Deer pause to sample a few as they come and go between food plots and resting areas.

We don't recommend planting an apple orchard to feed deer, because food plots are much more efficient. But if you're fortunate enough to have "wild" apple trees on your property, do what you can to keep them healthy and producing fruit.

Don't underestimate the importance of wooded areas to deer, and don't underestimate how much quality habitat you can

Woods Working — TSI

create in the woods. Most of our clients don't do enough work on their wooded areas, even though woodlands are every bit as important to creating quality wildlife habitat as fields and food plots. Best of all, you don't need a lot of fancy tractors and farm implements to achieve your goals. A $500 investment in cutting gear will get the habitat-improvement ball rolling. For that price, you should be able to buy an ax, a few wedges and a semi-professional chainsaw. You'll also need safety chaps, eye and ear protection, and a helmet to protect you from potentially terrible accidents.

Photo by Charles J. Alsheimer

Chapter VIII

Logging On

You're riding the NorthCountry tram down a woodland road through a mixed oak, hickory and maple forest. Every 40 yards is an 18- to 22-inch stump. About 30 feet from each stump lies a severed treetop heavily browsed by deer. In the protection of these treetops, dozens of oak seedlings stretch for daylight. This scene is duplicated throughout this 100-acre stand of hardwoods, and is the result of a select-cut logging operation five years before. Oak regeneration is everywhere. Acorns abound on the ground. Other than an occasional treetop and stump, one would not know loggers had been here. They did their job well. But this was not always the case. Twelve years before, loggers made a mess and virtually destroyed another wooded area on the demo site. We learned our lessons on logging the first time.

Make no mistake: Logging does not have to be a four-letter word. Timber harvests have a significant place in habitat management, and should be viewed as a vital tool that provides cash while improving habitat. Unfortunately, logging has developed a

This landowner is smiling now, but he won't be so happy when he realizes how difficult, if not impossible, it is to repair this heavy-equipment rut. This kind of damage can and must be prevented.

questionable-to-bad reputation in recent years. Some logging practices have scarred woods with irreparable damage. Some operators have been unscrupulous and taken advantage of landowners. For the most part, the bad rap has been well-deserved.

However, with the right approach, logging can be a positive management tool. Money from timber sales can be used to purchase equipment like tractors and field implements. Timber harvests can also provide that much-desired road network on your property for free. When you realize you would pay $75 to $125 per hour to rent a bulldozer, it's easy to see how you can get thousands of dollars of access roads as a byproduct of a large logging operation.

Finally, logging can improve habitat dramatically. It thins overcrowded timber and drops treetops, allowing daylight to break through to the ground for the first time in years. Wildlife habitat springs up everywhere as cover and food abound. Best of all, you're getting paid for the job, not paying to have it done.

Logging On

To maximize logging's benefits, you must put on your thinking cap before beginning. Consult your overall management plan to review your goals and objectives. Once you understand how logging fits into your program and you're relatively certain you want to proceed, hire a consulting forester. Share your plan with him so he can help you make critical decisions. A qualified forester ensures you get a good price for your logs. Because most foresters work on a percentage basis, they strive to ensure you get top dollar for your timber by putting the job out to competitive bids. Also, they make sure logging roads are laid out correctly, and left in a serviceable condition after the job is complete.

Once you and your forester agree on your goals, he marks the trees to be cut and bids out the job. Once the bids are in, he

Logging usually improves deer habitat dramatically. It creates food, cover and open spaces. This buck, and others like him, will use this cut-over area for at least eight to 10 years.

reviews them and presents a recommendation. He also steers you clear of fly-by-night loggers. The conventional wisdom is that consulting foresters more than pay for themselves, even with their commissions netted out. Their expertise is important and necessary. When shopping for a forester, check references and ask around for recommendations. This person is critical to your operation.

The services of a consulting forester are a huge asset in a logging operation. They help you get top dollar for your timber and ensure the work gets done correctly.

Make sure your forester understands your management goals. Most foresters are in the business of growing and harvesting timber, and some are not sympathetic to the needs of wildlife. We like to leave dead snag trees as nesting sites for birds and critters. Foresters usually remove snags because they can harbor diseases, but we think their value to wildlife usually outweighs those concerns. The occasional aggressive browse-cut is also attractive to wildlife, yet many foresters will not cut that heavily. A few extra trees removed from a 1-acre parcel can create a high-quality browse-cut that pays huge benefits to your program. When it comes to your woods, you're the boss. Remember that!

Logging On

The highest bidder is not always the best choice when selecting a cutter. Get references and inspect other jobs they have completed. Did they excessively damage existing trees while harvesting others? Did they drop large trees and crush smaller ones excessively? Also, did they damage large numbers of trees by "barking" them when skidding logs out of the woods? Trees with serious bark damage eventually rot because organisms attack the tree through the damaged area.

••
The highest bidder is not always the best choice when selecting a cutter. Get references and inspect other jobs they have completed.
••

Also, heavy equipment should not create impassable trenches and mud holes. Did they do a thorough job cleaning up? Most of these problems can be avoided if loggers show skill and care in the woods. They should leave it in better condition than they found it. You do not have to accept excessive damage from logging. Sure, some damage occurs, but it can be minimized and your woods will look good when they leave.

We have become so fussy that we request certain cutters for our property. We specify that one cutter, Roger Gee from the Two Rivers Timber Co. of Lindley, New York, do all our cutting. It's not that their other cutters are poor; we're just more comfortable with him because he is the best we've ever seen. He understands our management program and takes the time to do work we're happy with. He is also highly productive, so don't accept "productivity" excuses for sloppy work, and don't accept a discounted price for your timber just because you want it done right. "Careful" and "productive" are not mutually exclusive terms.

Timber management must be done carefully. It will take more than your lifetime for your woodlots to recover from a cutting. A sloppy logging job is like putting your life savings into the hands of a shoddy investor. Timber is part of your financial future. Spend extra time, do your research, and do the job right.

Neil followed four or five cutters around one summer running the clean-up bulldozer. Not all cutters are equally skilled and some are bad news. Roger Gee is an artist with a chainsaw, and fells trees exactly where they must go. He removes small trees in the path of those he is felling so the small ones are not left splintered and bent over. Because of his expertise, we have few damaged trees in our woods. Tops on the ground are all you see. Our woodlots are beautiful six months after the job is complete.

Skidders are huge machines, capable of damaging trees and roads. The man operating this skidder is skilled and careful not to damage our woodlands excessively.

Logging On

In contrast, about three years before we bought our land, a former owner logged our property. The loggers worked through 60 days of almost continuous bad weather and regularly damaged the woods with heavy equipment. We were not in a position at the time to shut down the logging, but we learned a lesson, and we have had to live with the results. Not all loggers are created equal.

Skidders and skidder operators are also a critical part of this equation. These huge machines can wreak havoc with your

• •
A logging contract should address the construction of logging roads, erosion measures on roads and hillsides, and how the woods should be left when the job is complete.
• •

woods by barking trees and creating mud holes. But short of logging with horses — an entirely acceptable practice, but difficult to find — skidders are a necessary part of the work. Like cutters, not all skidder operators are created equal. The best we have seen is Jim Bridge. Jim and his machine might be big, but he maneuvers it in our woods as if it's a Volkswagen Rabbit. He is mindful of our property, as is his cutting partner, Mike.

Your forester will draw up a contract addressing issues such as the construction of logging roads, erosion-prevention measures on roads and hillsides, and how the woods should be left when the job is complete. The contract should include the maximum height that tops and debris can be left on the ground, and specify that damaged trees should be removed and paid for. Splintered or broken trees and hangers, or "widow-makers," must be cut and dropped.

Logging roads are part of every job. After the job, they should be cleaned up, graded and have erosion-control measures installed. Planting deer forages not only provides food, but helps control erosion. This is where some loggers duck out. Set up a performance bond in escrow to ensure they stick around for the cleanup.

Often overlooked is a performance bond. A certain percentage — about 10 percent of the overall value of the timber — should be held by you to assure the loggers comply with the contract. That way, if they fail to clean up properly, or unreasonably damage your property, you're holding enough money to hire the work needed to put things right in the woods. Loggers hate this practice, but stick to your guns — especially if you don't know your loggers or haven't checked references. Even the best loggers require clean-up work. It usually requires several thousand dollars of bulldozer time to clean up the woods after a job. Holding their money is your insurance the work gets finished.

Done correctly, logging can be a great asset to you as a wildlife manager. Approach it as a business, and your wildlife and land will win.

Photo by Charles J. Alsheimer

Photo by Charles J. Alsheimer

Chapter IX

Food Plots for Feeding

The NorthCountry tram brings you through a narrow access road surrounded by poplar and white birch, but then you break into a clearing where the ground is lush and green. Like a giant football field, the food plot seems to go on forever. It could be hay or alfalfa, but a closer look indicates the field contains assorted rich stands of high-quality deer forages, brassicas to the right, clover and chicory to the left, and a mixture of both in the middle. No trees or irregular plantings interrupt the broad expanse. This field has been laid out to produce forage by the ton, and it feeds scores of white-tailed deer. You're looking at one of the feeding plots at the NorthCountry Demo Center. Six years before, this area was five acres of scrub brush. Hawthorne, gray dogwood and scrub pine were abundant. Deer bedded here and eked out a living on browse. That was before we launched our mission to provide high-quality food-plot forages for the deer.

Feeding food plots are designed and managed for agriculture, not hunting. The objective is to produce as much high-quality for-

Photo by Charles J. Alsheimer

This 5-acre feeding plot produces about 50 tons of 30-plus percent protein forage in one year. This keeps the 20-plus deer using it daily in good groceries year-round. Yes, even in winter.

age for deer as space permits. We lay out feeding plots for planting efficiency, which minimizes labor and maximizes our return per square foot worked. These fields usually cover three or more acres. Our agricultural practices are as close to being commercial as possible, including large equipment and commercial fertilizer and lime applications. We do this to save time and money, and yes, to feed deer. Every night these "destination feeding plots" are loaded with fat whitetails chomping down 30-plus percent protein forages. Deer from our property, as well as the neighbors' properties, aggressively seek out these forages for their evening meal, and spend most of the night on or near them. That's why we call them "destination plots."

Serious habitat managers usually want to increase the quality and quantity of deer forage on their property. This is the science

Food Plots for Feeding

Destination Feeding Food Plot

©NorthCountry Whitetails LLC 2002

This feeding food plot is laid out for efficient use of agricultural equipment. It covers three or more acres, and produces tons of highly nutritious forage. It will be planted with perennials and annuals for maximum productivity. Such sites are a favorite destination for whitetails on our property.

of food plots. A 1-acre high-quality food plot can produce up to 10 tons of 30-plus percent usable protein.

Plots of three or so acres can produce serious tonnage. Usable — i.e., digestible — protein is the key, because not all forages have the same digestibility to deer. For instance, most strains of alfalfa, which has a high stem content, are much less digestible for deer than most fine-stemmed clovers designed for whitetails.

Feeding food plots should be laid out to accommodate agricultural practices. Plots larger than two acres usually require farm implements. They're too large for ATV equipment. They should be located in areas accessible to farm equipment. For years at the Demo Center, we hand-spread fertilizer and lime on remote food plots. We finally got smart and developed a network of heavy-duty roads that allowed us to bring in tractors and commercial fertil-

Access roads allow the commercial spreading of lime and fertilizer. Each year we save thousands of dollars and hundreds of hours of back-breaking labor by hiring commercial spreaders. This UAP spreading truck will cover a 5-acre plot in no time.

Undesirable grasses are ever present in food plots, and can quickly take over a quality plot. We use a grass-specific herbicide like Poast to keep grasses in check. It will not harm our broadleafs like brassicas, chicory and clover.

izer spreaders. By the time we had the road developed, some of the plots had expanded into 5-acre parcels. A lime truck can spread 10 tons of lime in about 30 minutes. This lime costs just over $30 per ton. Before using commercial spreaders, we bought lime in pellet form. It came in 50-pound bags we could handle manually. We hauled it in a pickup truck, and transported it by ATV to a small spinner-type spreader. The process took a weekend to do the same work a lime truck accomplishes in a half-hour. Even worse was the cost. Pellet lime cost more than $120 per ton, not to mention the intense labor. Spreading 20 tons a year cost a lot of money and was physically ruinous. That's why access roads are needed to work large plots efficiently.

Today, with BioLogic's ph Fertilizer, we can do the same work in half the time for $70 per acre. The combination of lime and fertilzier in one pellet is a real labor and time saver. The only down side to the pH Fertilzier is it is a short-term pH solution. That is, the lime only raises the pH for one growing season. By the end of the season, you are pretty much back to where you started on the pH scale. It's great for giving plots a jump start and a mid-season boost but traditional aggricultural lime will still be required to keep pH levels up year in and year out.

Feeding food plots should be laid out to accommodate long, straight equipment runs and the large turning radii of medium-sized (30 to 60 hp) tractors pulling 10- to 16-foot wide implements. This is best accomplished by designing large rectangular- or square-shaped plots. Uneven edges and islands of trees add interest and aesthetics, but they interfere with efficient cultivation.

In order to meet your goal of providing as much high-quality forage for deer as possible, you must use proven agricultural practices such as liming and fertilizing, as well as grass and weed control. We now understand why most growers use modern chemical treatments. We resisted chemical weed control for a time, preferring to go "organic," but by the late 1990s we accepted chemical treatments of our food plots. We researched the chemicals we use, and believe they're the only way to go, given our goals, objectives and available time.

Before planting, we use a herbicide like Roundup® or Ultra® to kill weeds and grasses. If left unchecked, they will compete with and eventually destroy a high-quality forage stand. Midway though the growing season, we apply a herbicide such as Poast® to reduce grasses and keep the food plots producing lush clovers, chicories and brassicas that deer covet. Poast® does not harm broadleaf cultivars like clover, brassicas and chicory. Chemical treatments are a huge plus to our program. When treated right, our plots last for years.

Food Plots for Feeding

Steps to Food-Plot Construction

The steps for creating quality food plots are the same as steps for most agriculture. First, take soil samples by removing 12 pint-size scoops with a shovel or soil-sample auger. Follow an "X" pattern across the plot, and put all dirt in one pail. Use the topsoil or subsoil on each plot. Stir and mix the soil, and then remove 1½ cups and place it in a poly-bag for analysis. You want the average of a good-cross section of the plot. Use an extension service or university, and tell them what you intend to plant — clover, chicory, etc. They will recommend the amount of lime and type of fertilizer to apply per acre.

In most Northern areas, soils are pH deficient on the acidic side. Soils of 4.5 are very acidic, and a 6.5 pH is moderately acidic. A 7 is neutral. If your sample test comes back at 5.2, the acidity is

Soil tests are invaluable. Without them, you have no map to follow when applying lime and fertilizer. Do not skip this step!

binding nutrients in the soil. The nutrients are there, but the plants cannot use them. Applying lime raises the pH and allows plants to use nutrients more efficiently. When we apply fertilizer on a low-pH food plot, the plants can use only a portion of the fertilizer. A 5.2 pH food plot might waste 40 percent of the fertilizer applied. Lime is vital, but it might take three or more years of lime applications to raise highly acidic soil to the neutral range. Biologic markets a quick-release product called "pHertilizer," which is comprised of quick-acting lime and fertilizer. It's a great way to accelerate plantings while slower-acting limes gradually start working. The pHertilizer product, however, does not maintain the pH level more than one growing season. You must use it every time you plant, and maybe once during the growing season, too. We've had great results using it in autumn plantings of attractants.

Using a herbicide such as Roundup® first is more efficient than plowing and disking first to rid food plots of weeds. It is also more friendly to the soil as disturbed soil is prone to erosion

Food Plots for Feeding

Common indicators in the North of acidic soils are moss, blueberries and conifers. Oaks are also associated with acidic soils. If your dollars are limited, buy lime first and then fertilize when you have the cash.

After determining the soil's pH, apply herbicides and/or cultivate to kill weeds and grasses. We apply Roundup® first. Plowing and disking weeds is not as effective as applying herbicides first, because you get almost instant regrowth when you plow and disk. Killing weeds with herbicides is more efficient than cultivating, and that's why most commercial growers use them.

After the herbicide does its job, which takes about one week, turn the soil with a plow or disk to work dead matter into the soil and break up dirt clods for a smooth seedbed. This ensures max-

This neat food plot has just been cultipacked. It is now ready for seed to be spread. No air pockets or dirt clods will inhibit germination and root development.

imum germination. We smooth and pack the surface with a roller or cultipacker before we seed to remove air pockets, which inhibit seeds and roots. Packing the surface also creates a smooth surface for spreading seeds, and allows the soil to better hold moisture and heat. Thus, a firm seedbed improves seed germination and produces a better stand of forage.

It's now time for the Weather Channel. It's no accident that farmers have watched the weather for eternity. Ideally, a gentle, day-long rain will arrive as soon as you finish seeding. Rain and soil moisture are critical to success. The worst scenario is germination followed by drought. This is a fatal to any kind of crop. Timing your seeding pays dividends. Of course, you can play the weather only a few days at a time, but it's worth a try. Beyond that, it's all up to Mother Nature. But remember, nothing happens without moisture.

With rain in the future, it's time to broadcast your seed. Today's food-plot blends list the specific recommended amounts per acre. This information is found on the bag. Follow the manufacturer's recommendations. It's

An old-fashioned "whirly gig" hand-spreader does the job with little wasted seed. ATV spreaders are quicker, but must be used carefully so as not to apply too much or too little seed.

tempting to exceed the recommended level, because if one bag is good, two must be better, right? Dead wrong! If you apply too much seed, the now overcrowded plants produce less forage per acre. On the other hand, don't try to stretch your dollars too far. Sow too few seeds and weeds will encroach between the plants. If you're confident in your soil and its preparation, plant as recom-

••••••••••••••••••••••••••••••••••••••
Do not hand-cast the seed. This is wasteful and creates uneven stands. Hand-casting is for the movies.
••••••••••••••••••••••••••••••••••••••

mended. If you don't expect good germination or if deer denisty it high, plant a bit more.

High-quality seed can be expensive and your dollars will stretch further if you proceed carefully. If you don't have an expensive seed drill — and most people don't — get a small, food-type scale to measure a quarter-acre of seed. Measure 25 by 50 yards and spread the seed one-quarter acre at a time. Better to trickle your seed and go over the same ground a couple of times than to blow it out the first 20 yards. Don't pour too much seed into the hopper all at once, especially if you're using a large-capacity seeder. Trust us, $100 of seed can disappear in less than a minute if you set it wrong.

If you're walking between two points, and assuming 2.8 mph is the average walking speed, an over-the-shoulder or hand-held seeder can be very effective. Some hand-held seeders cost less than $20. Also consider an ATV seeder. We like the one manufactured by Monroe Tufline. It is wheel-driven, and has a large capacity and exact settings. It also can be adjusted to spread right, left or both directions.

Do not hand-cast the seed. This is wasteful and creates uneven stands. Hand-casting is for the movies. Also realize an acre is often difficult to judge. In rough terms, a football field, which is 50 yards wide and 100 yards long, covers about one acre. Hand-held measuring wheels are useful for precise calculations. Laser range-finders designed for hunting are also great for laying out food plots. We use the Bushnell model. Now you have two excuses to buy one.

After seeding, run the cultipacker once over the food plot. A roller also works well. If you're planting clover, rape, chicory or other small seeds, don't bury them too deeply. They should be in the top quarter-inch of soil. Some people like to disk after seeding, but we don't. A disk usually puts seeds too deep into the soil, causing most of it to be lost. If you cannot "contact" the seed to the soil by rolling, we believe it's better to leave the job to Mother Nature. A good rain does a perfect job. The small, versatile ATV "Plotmaster" does a great job of seedbed preparation and rolling. We use it on our smaller plots. Plotmaster also makes a larger product for tractors, which

A "utilization cage" in each plot is a must. These tell you how much your plot is being used by feeding deer. Too much or too little use might mean problems. Twelve feet of 3-foot high welded wire and a wooden stake make a fine cage.

Food Plots for Feeding

we look forward to trying. On tiny food plots, we sometimes drive the seed in with our John Deere Gator, which has balloon turf tires. It sets seeds firmly into the soil.

Utilization Cages Tell the Story

After planting, place some utilization cages in your food plot. Make them from 1 x 2-inch welded wire, 3 feet in diameter and 3 feet tall. A 12-foot length of the wire mesh works nicely. Be sure to stake cages securely, because deer and other wildlife bump them. This tool helps you gauge how much the plot is being used, and indicates how many more plots you should plant, if any. If six weeks pass and you notice the food plot's vegetation is 18 inches high inside the cage and 2 to 3 inches tall outside, you have high deer use.

This is good news and bad. The good news is the stuff is growing and deer love it. The bad news is that by winter, there won't be much left. You should look to plant more food plots or thin your herd dramatically. A deer will eat 1¾ tons of food per year, with much of that coming from food plots, assuming you have them. Paying attention to how intensively deer use food plots and browse areas reveals a lot about the herd and its needs.

People touring our Demo Center are often surprised we don't grow corn in our food plots. Why not? We don't believe in corn food plots. Corn is a one-month wonder in our region, and does little for antler growth and body size. It nourishes whitetails for a few weeks in autumn, and then it's gone. Other plants produce forage year-round. Also, every farmer in our county plants corn. Some leave it standing all winter.

We prefer a mixture of high-protein forages that stay available all year, from early spring through winter. We want to meet the nutritional needs of lactating does, nursing fawns and bucks growing antlers. BioLogic's New Zealand blends of clover, chicory and brassicas are our favorites. These blends grow low and dense, and are low in stem material, or lignin. Their density keeps down competing weeds. They're designed to be grazed, and as such, mature at different times of the year.

We also don't plant cattle forages like alfalfa, red clover and tall white ladino, because these are grown to be chopped or baled and fed dry. They are high in coarse stem materials and lignin,

> *By mid-May, our clovers are producing major tonnage, and are starting to get ahead of the deer herd. The chicory kicks in shortly after the clover, so by mid-June we're often knee-high in clover and chicory.*

which deer do not digest as well as cattle do. We call clovers that grow hip-high on fibrous stems — which deer can't efficiently use — "feel-good" clovers. You feel good when you walk by the stand because of its height and appearance, but that's about the end of it. "Stemmy" forages grow that high because deer don't care to eat them when more digestible cultivars are growing nearby.

A food-plot program should have some food plots or fields dedicated to producing tons of nutrition. Done correctly, these plots should produce nutritious forage year-round, even in the North. On the Demo Center, spring green-up starts in mid-April. Our clover blends — BioLogic blends have four or more clovers in each blend — kick in then and are heavily used by pregnant does. By mid-May, all of our clovers are producing major tonnage,

Food Plots for Feeding

and are starting to get ahead of the herd. The chicory kicks in shortly after the clover, so by mid-June we're often knee-high in clover and chicory.

We then begin a mowing program to control weeds and keep the plots fresh. We mow the top one-third of the plants when they reach about 12 inches tall. During the growing season, we can mow on a Saturday and by the next Wednesday the plot looks like it never saw a mower. We mow all summer to control weeds and keep our plots fresh. The only time we don't mow is during dry spells. Speaking of dry spells, chicory is the secret weapon for dry conditions. It has an incredibly long taproot, which allows it to thrive in drought-like conditions. In 2002 we endured the second driest summer in New York history, and our clovers resembled toast for 45 days. Chicory thrived the entire time.

Photo by Charles J. Alsheimer

This band of bucks is chowing down after a long, difficult breeding season. They're in the process of regaining the weight they lost during the rut. This is why we call brassicas the secret weapon of Northern food plots.

The only trouble was, by the end of the drought, we could barely find a chicory plant on the place. The deer had mowed almost every one of them to the ground. Even so, they kept growing and reappeared when the clover came back with the rain. When the deer zeroed in again on the clover, the chicory got its chance to thrive once more.

We plant brassicas at the Demo Center in spring and fall. The deer key on brassicas after a hard freeze or the first snow. This usually occurs in mid-November. The whitetails paw through snow all winter to reach the 8 to 10 tons of brassicas we grow per acre. Some people get upset when deer ignore brassicas in summer and early fall. We celebrate this avoidance because it means that much more will be available in late fall and winter.

Our brassicas are pretty much cleared out by mid-March. This leaves the deer about a month to make a living without our help. We notice them hanging around south-facing springs and seeps during early spring, taking advantage of nature's earliest green-up.

Feeding deer is important to our program. Our harvested deer have increased in weight about 20 percent from the time we started weighing them in the early 1990s. Their racks are noticeably larger, too.

Obviously, no deer-management program is complete without thinking about year-round nutrition. Therein lies the beauty of serious food plots.

⟶

Photo by Charles J. Alsheimer

Photo by Charles J. Alsheimer

Chapter X

Food Plots for Hunting

You have left the NorthCountry tram and are walking down a winding 6-foot-wide path that opens into a half-acre clearing. This field is carpeted in rich, ankle deep wheat, brassicas and clover. This clearing has an irregular shape, with several hunter-hiding pines on the fringe. Man-made licking branches have been strategically placed within bow range of two well-hidden tree stands. Impenetrable brush is piled downwind behind the stands. The brush piles ensure no buck can get downwind of a hunter during a prevailing westerly wind.

The stage is set for success. But a year before, this setup was just another half-acre of brush and cover. It was part of an 80-acre overgrown pasture and almost impossible to hunt because of its density.

Hunting food plots are laid out differently than feeding plots. They're usually smaller — 1/4 to 3/4 acres — irregularly shaped, and planted to attract deer during the hunting season. Cover juts into the plot to take advantage of wind direction and maximize hunter concealment. These peninsulas of cover proide close-range encounters for hunters, and add visual interest to the plot. Good hunting plots look like they've been there forever because they blend into the landscape. While feeding plots are laid out for agricultural efficiency, hunting plots are set up for close encounters with game.

Take Your Time Laying it Out

Before creating and setting up a hunting plot, it's vital to select your hunting location. Analyze how deer move in and out of the area by studying their trails. Early spring is a good time for this. Consider prevailing winds during the hunting season, and leave concealment cover intact. Consider bedding areas and anticipate a deer's route from the bedding area to the plot area. Study wind factors and weather patterns the

Deer love edge environments with their assortments of cover and foods. Good hunting plots have irregular edges, with scrapes and licking branches within easy range of the stand.

Food Plots for Hunting

Before starting bulldozer or brushhog work, carefully lay out the plot's shape and size. Plan where to pile up the brush beforehand to make plot construction easier. The piled brush should be "hidden" and used to channel deer movement.

hunting season before you lay out your plot. In our location, prevailing winds come from the west, varying southwest to northwest. We set up most of our plots to take advantage of these winds. Spend time at these sites with wind directional tools, such as Windfloaters™ from API Treestands. These little tufts of milkweed-like material are great for studying wind currents. Be sure to release them from tree-stand height. Better yet, release them from the tree you wish to hunt from. Smoke bombs work well, too, as do some light powders. Besides testing prevailing winds, it's also important to understand how morning and evening thermal drafts affect drifting scents.

Pay attention to how you approach your hunting plot. Deer usually try to approach smaller food plots with the wind in their face, but deer-blocking wind-rows created by felled trees and piled brush channel deer through ambush sites. We always try to use wind-rows of piled brush to prevent deer from entering the plot downwind of a bow stand. Wind-rows get there with the help of a bulldozer or chainsaw.

Once you've studied the area, begin laying out the location and shape of your plot, and where you'll place your stands.

•••

Enclosed tower stands are weatherproof, and can accommodate heaters. Be sure they can hold two people. A comfortable enclosed stand is an ideal way to hunt with a beginner or friend.

•••

Whenever possible, locate your stands in dense, dark trees. Conifers are excellent hunting trees because they provide concealment and shelter from the elements.

Choosing a Stand

When good hiding trees are unavailable, some hunters prefer an enclosed tower stand. These stands can be particularly effective for gun-hunters, and when no suitable trees are available and ground hunting is impractical. Tower stands can be bought or made from 4 x 4 posts, plywood and 2 x 4's. Enclosed blinds like these are weatherproof, and can accommodate heaters. They're extremely comfortable. Be sure the stand can hold two people, because this is an ideal way to hunt with a beginner or good friend.

Food Plots for Hunting

On the other hand, enclosed tower stands tend to be permanent and somewhat obtrusive. Tuck them away in the edge of the plot so they don't stick out like a sore thumb. Use trees and brush to disguise the silhouette. It will look more natural if it's camouflaged. For a year-round camo blind, go to a rural dump right after Christmas and look for artificial Christmas trees. Collect the Christmas-tree boughs and recycle them by attaching them to the sides of the box or blind. These synthetic evergreen boughs last for years and make the stand look like an evergreen clump. They can make your blind become one with the surrounding cover.

This hunter is about to experience the benefits of hunting over food plots.

The most common stands are hang-ons, ladder-stands and, of course, climbers. Be sure not to cut down trees in strategic locations that will support or hide your tree stands. We don't build permanent stands into trees. They not only damage trees and are unsightly, but mature deer learn their whereabouts and avoid them. Check the wind 12 to 16 feet up in these trees with Floaters™. Two or three tree stands per plot are not too many. Each should be set up for a different wind direction. Set them early in the year and be selective about removing limbs that aid concealment. Craig likes clear shooting and always cuts off too many limbs. As a result, he often gets "made" by wary deer. Neil, on the other hand, being more agile and easier to hide, prunes little and blends in with the tree he's hunting in. Once you cut limbs, they're gone forever unless you're handy with bailing wire and limb loppers.

Don't forget ground-blind strategies. When no trees are suitable for hunting, and ground blinds are your only option, lay out the plot with that in mind. At other times, a ground blind can be a backup or strategic choice that is used perhaps once

Food plots designed for hunting attract deer at all times of the day, because they often bed within yards of the plots. Always sneak in and out, and don't be afraid to hunt them at odd times of the day.

This nasty, dirt-packed brush should not be left in a "halo" around the plot. Push it into one or two corridors as far from the plot as possible. You don't want to sit in a stand staring at ugly brush all day. Hide your trash. Your goal is to create a plot that looks like it's 5 years old just one month after it's planted.

a year to ambush a buck that's wary of your tree-stand locations. Be creative when laying out the food plot, and plan multiple ambush sites so you can hunt in various winds. On some hunting plots, wind conditions might not be appropriate for certain stands and — based on which days you're able to hunt — you might have to avoid them for two or three years. Don't force the issue. Wait until you get the perfect wind to move in and kill that trophy whitetail!

Once a chainsaw or bulldozer removes a piece of cover, it will never be there again. Plan carefully. Plan in advance. Pick sites for your plots with hunting in mind. Hunting plots are often laid out in a wooded or heavy-brush environment. A bulldozer is usually needed to clear the ground. When using a moderate-sized bulldozer, plan on at least eight hours of bulldozer work per acre of ground to be cleared. Lighter brush can be mowed with a stout rotary mower and 30 hp tractor. Mowing and liming the brushed area for a couple of years takes care of all of the brush and sweetens your soil. Plant food-plot forage the second or third year, and you will have a killer plot.

Create Good-Looking Plots

Aesthetics should be considered in creating all food plots. After all, you will spend hours in those locations, and most of

• •
Aesthetics should be considered in creating food plots. After all, you will spend hours in those locations, and most of us would rather be surrounded by beauty than something that resembles a construction site.
• •

us would rather be surrounded by beauty than something that resembles a construction site. A skilled bulldozer operator can hide debris by pushing it into the brush on a diagonal line to the field. Initially, you should push the brush pile at least 30 yards from the plot's edge. That way it won't back up into the edge of the plot. Clearing debris is nasty work, and it's tempting to leave several piles around the edges. It takes more work, but we suggest creating no more than two piles, and hiding those piles by pushing them as far from the plot as possible. A bulldozer operator unfamiliar with food-plot conditions will want to leave all debris banked around the food plot like a halo. This is ugly, and it blocks the deer's entrance and exit

Food Plots for Hunting

trails. Tell the bulldozer operator what you want beforehand so he can lay it out. A month after its construction, a food plot should look like it has been there for five years. Paying attention to details now reaps dividends as you sit hour after hour watching the plot.

As a bowhunter, you must be on high alert when hunting small food plots. If you wait for deer to enter the plot before drawing your bow, it might be too late. They might hear you or catch your movement. During the 2001 rut, we knew some quality bucks were working near a small hunting plot. Craig was in his stand 20 minutes when he heard a deer marching along a trail that paralleled a food plot. As expected, the deer met a wind-row and followed it into the field. Craig suspected it was a buck, but waited for it to enter the field before grabbing

This hunting plot was built two weeks before this photo was taken. It is irregularly shaped. Hunting trees still stand along its edges. The brush has been hidden, and the plot is simply beautiful.

his bow. Before Craig could react, the 120-class buck was 15 yards away, and bowhunter and quarry were face to face. Craig managed to get his bow and draw it slowly, but just as he was aligning his pin and peep sight, the deer snorted and ran. This was an amateur performance by someone who knows better than to get caught flat-footed with the bow on its hanger! Be alert and get your bow ready as soon as you suspect deer.

Neil's Signature Plots that Work

Over the years, Neil has sited dozens of hunting food plots. He has also studied which types of plot layouts work well for bowhunting, and which don't quite cut it. Remember, the purpose of a hunting plot is to attract and kill deer, not just attract and feed them. Neil has taken small hunting-plot designs to another level of mastery, and developed a series of plots we call Neil Dougherty's Signature Plots. These layouts have produced dozens of deer over the years, and at least one of these designs should work in almost any hunting food-plot setting you have on your property.

It's important to note we do not recommend round food plots. We can't think of one application where a round plot is the ticket. They're difficult to plant, and do little to control deer movements. Round works in ponds, but not in hunting food plots. Square plots aren't much better.

Before tackling a hunting plot, take time to study the wind, the lay of the land, and deer-movement patterns. Next, study the following diagrams and utilization criteria to determine which setups would work best for you on your property. Duplicating one or more of these designs will pay dividends when that trophy of a lifetime pays a visit.

Food Plots for Hunting

Food plots are usually sited in one of two ways. Sometimes you create your own plots from relatively uniform cover, and sometimes you use existing open spaces created by farming. The first three plots we describe on the following pages fit the former category and allow you to maximize creativity. However, they require serious equipment for clearing brush. At the minimum, a stout rotary mower is required. More than likely, you will also need a bulldozer.

Neil's See-Through Hourglass Food Plot©

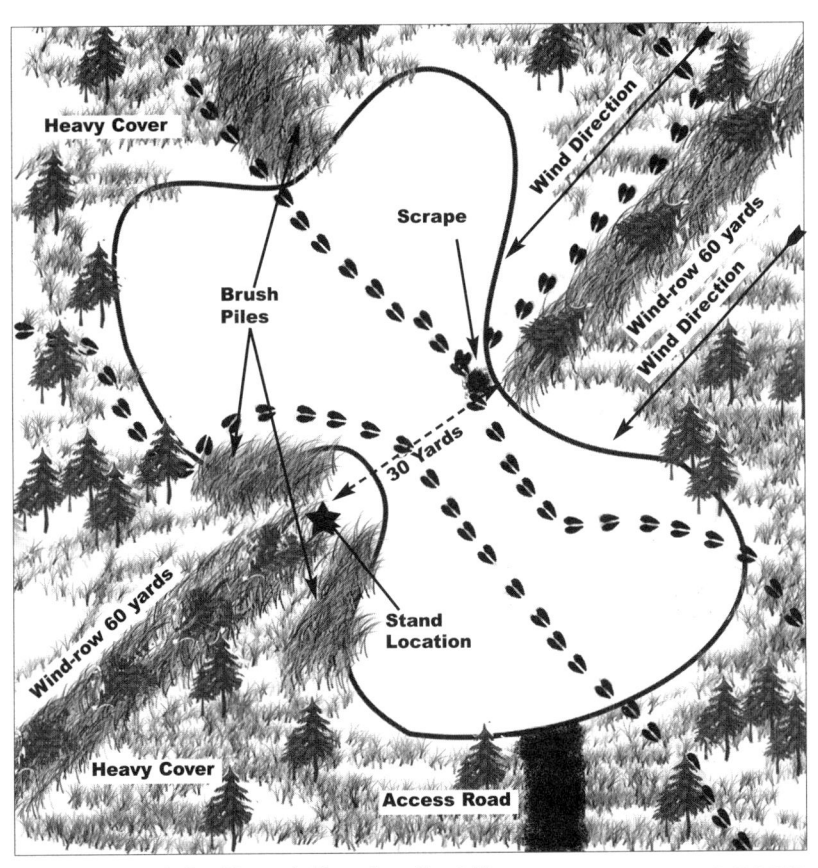

Neil Dougherty's See-Through Hourglass Food Plot ©NorthCountry Whitetails LLC 2002

The hourglass plot's unique design allows you to create a larger-than-normal bowhunting food plot. Although most bowhunting food plots should be less than a half-acre in size, the hourglass can cover up to an acre. Planted with a mix of brassicas, clover and chicory, this plot can create nearly 10 tons of forage.

• •
The food plot's neck serves as a stopping place for most deer. Not only does it have a scrape and licking branch, but the neck also affords deer their best visibility of the entire plot.
• •

The key to Neil's See-Through Hourglass design is its neck that is 30 yards wide. This is where your stand should be located. Two stands can be placed there to take advantage of different winds. Licking branches and mock scrapes should also be located in the neck. It's also important that deer be able to see that the neck doesn't dead-end. That is, deer should be able to see some open space beyond the neck, no matter where they are on the plot. This piques their curiosity and draws them into the neck to see what lies beyond.

The neck of the food plot will serve as a stopping place for most deer. Not only because of the signposts — the scrape and licking branch — you placed there, but because the neck affords deer their best visibility of the entire plot. Deer relax more when they can see what's ahead as well as behind. Keep deer from approaching behind your stand by blocking that direction with brush-piled wind-rows. Deer will learn to approach the plot from another direction. Wind-rows should also be used on the upwind side to direct the deer's approach.

Food Plots for Hunting

Locating the hourglass plot in thick cover increases deer visitations during hunting hours. Mature bucks spend most of their daylight hours in thick cover, but will visit this plot for a quick mouthful of food or to check for does.

Neil's Boomerang Bushwhack Plot©

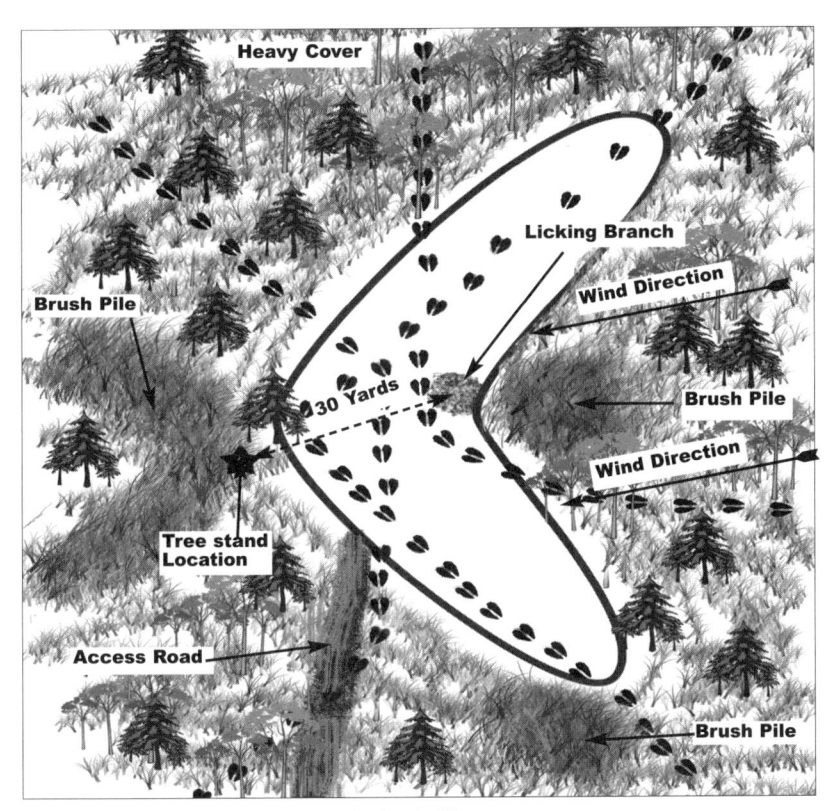

Neil Dougherty's Boomerang Bushwhack Plot ©NorthCountry Whitetails LLC 2002

Neil's Boomerang Bushwhack food plot adapts better to smaller areas than the hourglass plot. In particular, it works in narrower bands of cover, and generally covers a half-acre or less when set up for bowhunting. It's often planted with an annual blend of wheat, clover and brassicas, with the mix timed to reach peak palatability during the hunting season.

The key to the boomerang is the plot's ability to intercept multiple deer trails, and once deer enter the plot, to draw them through the elbow. The draw occurs because the gentle curve of the elbow reveals additional open space with each step the deer takes. Deer do not see the far end of the boomerang until they're in the elbow's curve.

The elbow, of course, is where the bushwhack takes place. Place your mock scrapes and licking branches on the elbow's upwind side 25 yards from the stand. Place brush piles to block deer from entering the plot downwind of the stand. Another brush pile or wind-row should be located opposite your stand to keep deer from cutting the corner. When deer cut corners through the brush, you lose shooting opportunities.

Like the hourglass, the boomerang is best located in thick, brushy areas.

Neil's Long Shot "S"©

Another versatile plot that can be created in thick cover is Neil's Long Shot "S" food plot. This plot works well for bow- or gun-hunters because it allows gun-hunters to spot deer at

• •
The Long Shot S food plot is about 20 yards wide, and its length is determined by topography and how far you're willing to shoot. Its distinctive feature is a bulge in the "S" itself.
• •

longer ranges while concentrating deer in one easy-to-hunt location for bowhunters. It is especially effective when located

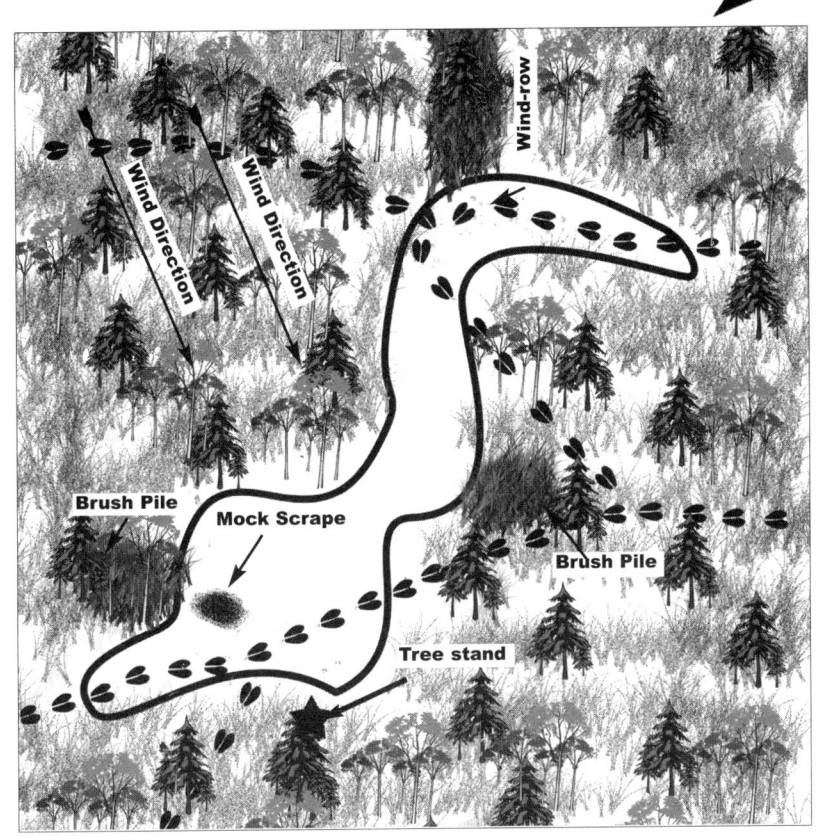

Neil Dougherty's Long-Shot "S" Plot ©NorthCountry Whitetails LLC 2002

in funnels and crossings. It also allows you to hunt long, narrow strips of brush, which are often found in farm country.

A *Long Shot S* food plot is about 20 yards wide, and its length is determined by topography and the maximum distance you'll shoot. Its distinctive feature is a bulge somewhere on the "S." The bulge is about 30 yards across in the spot where you bowhunt. It features licking branches, mock scrapes and deer-blocking brush piles downwind of the stand. This is the one spot on the entire "S" where deer tend to congregate, and it's also the spot where cruising bucks are sure to check out.

Even though this plot is long and stretches conveniently from Point A to Point B, don't use it as your transportation route. Human traffic on this food plot will ruin it for hunting in a hurry. This plot is best planted with long-lasting perennials because its irregular shape makes cultivation difficult.

Topography often dictates food-plot design. This is especially true in farm country, which is often checkerboarded with squares and rectangles of alternating woods and fields, with an occasional brush-lot thrown in for good measure. Straight edges and right angles are everywhere, as are abrupt transitions between cover types.

The food plots described in the next few pages take advantage of topographical features and — as such — are relatively easy to build.

Neil's Strip Stake Out Food Plot©

Neil's Strip Stake Out plots follow the topography, especially existing woods and thick cover. They're very effective when used as a food source between woods and fields or woods and brush. For these plots, you create a long, narrow — about 35 x 75 yards — strip adjoining an area where deer are comfortable, like a woods or brushy area. The trick is to get deer to enter the strip where you can get a bow shot.

Study access trails and manipulate the cover by creating log or brushy wind-rows around the plot. Woodlots adjoining fields often have wire fences where the woods meets the field. Look for gaps in the fence as likely places for deer to cross. If the fence has too many gaps, consider fixing it. Plant forages with an eye toward peak palatability, which pays huge bene-

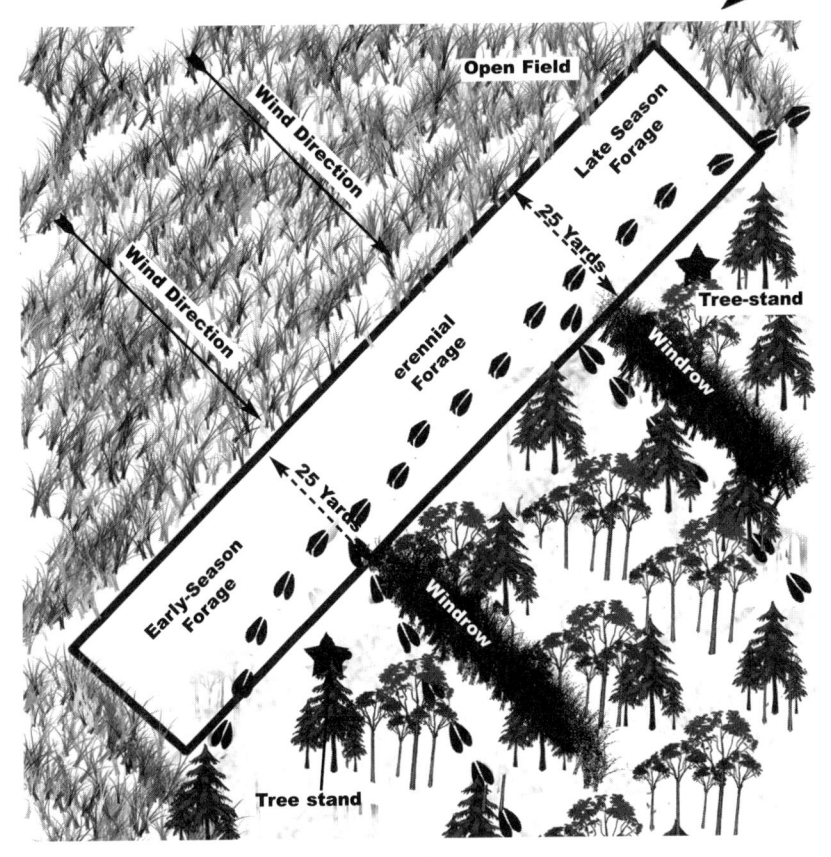

Neil Dougherty's Strip Stake Out Food Plot ©NorthCountry Whitetails LLC 2002

fits. Knowing which forages deer prefer during different phases of the hunting season help you determine stand sites.

Good shooting is often had 30 to 50 yards back into the cover, because mature bucks often scent-check the plot downwind from inside the cover. Get downwind of his scent-check trail and you'll have him. Don't overhunt these types of plots, because deer quickly learn to shy away from tree-stand setups along field edges. Climbing stands work well for these setups.

Neil's Corner Converger Food Plot

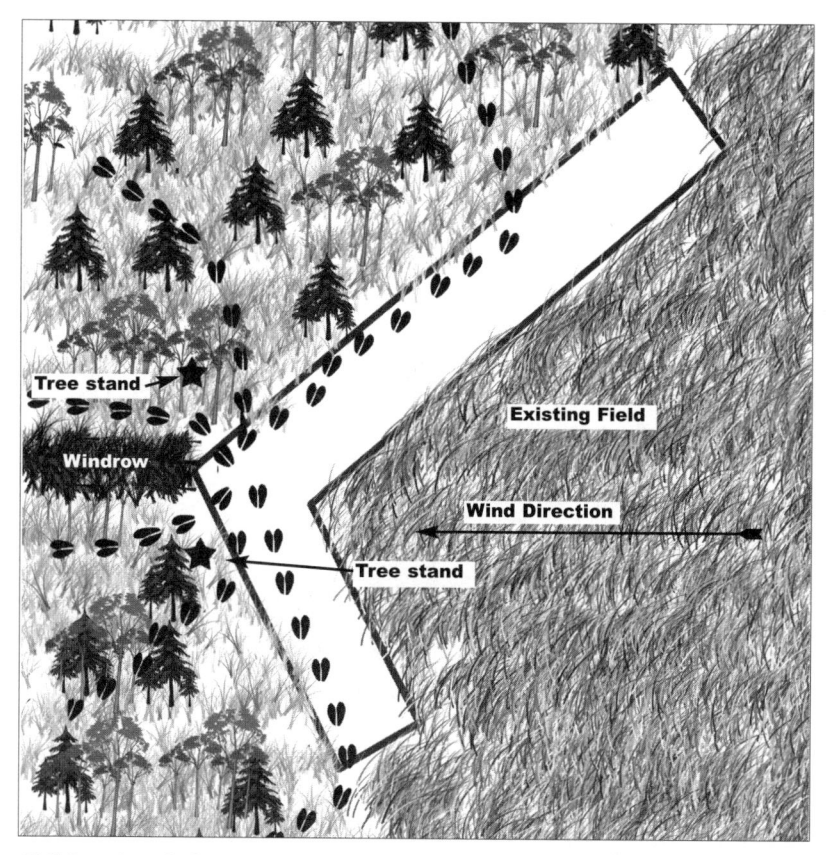

Neil Dougherty's Corner Converger Food Plot ©NorthCountry Whitetails LLC 2002

Corners where different covers meet have always been deer hotspots. They really heat up when planted with food-plot forages. The Corner Converger design makes the inside corners of fields hunting hotspots by concentrating deer. This design should not exceed 70 yards on the long leg and 30 yards on the short leg. The width should not exceed 25 yards. Sunlight-shading branches that overhang the food plot should be trimmed before planting.

One key to this plot is a wind-row that extends into the woods or brush to channel deer into the corner. The second key is planting the plot with forages that achieve peak palatability during the hunting season. Ideally, the existing field's forages will have long lost their appeal to deer. A good example would be a food plot full of brassicas next to a farmer's alfalfa field. The brassicas become very attractive just as the alfalfa loses its appeal in cold weather. Bucks will check out the plot from the cover of the woods. But instead of skirting the plot, they will follow the wind-row into the corner ambush.

Neil's Comfortable Corner

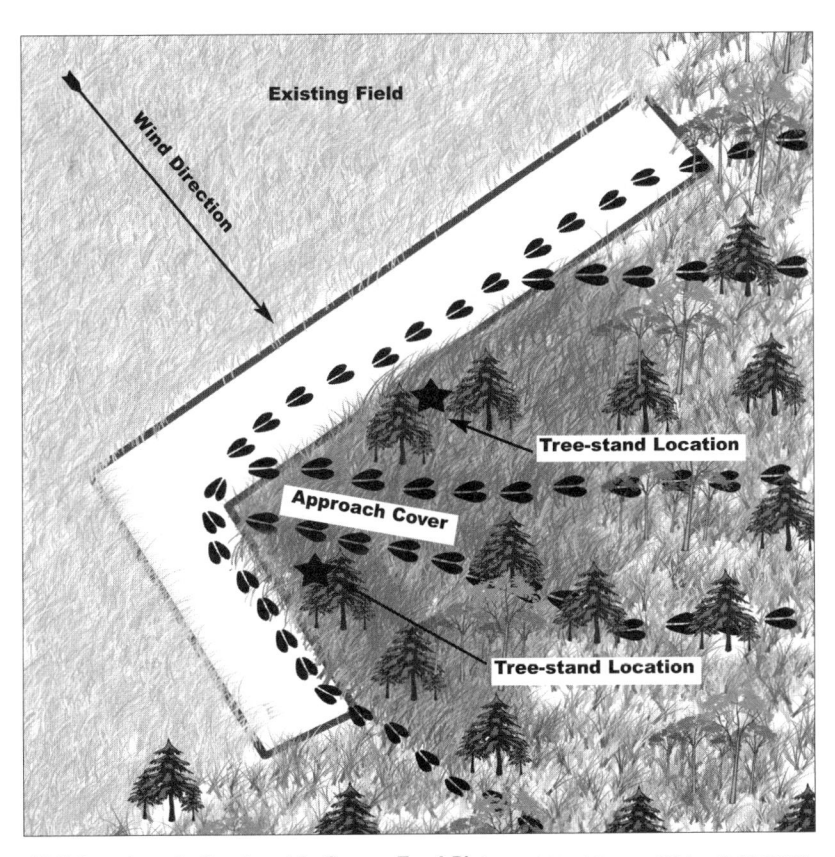

Neil Dougherty's Comfortable Corner Food Plot ©NorthCountry Whitetails LLC 2002

The Comfortable Corner is designed to concentrate deer on the cover side — usually a woodlot — of a food plot. Hunters have known for years that corners like this make good ambush sites as deer travel the edges of cover. The Comfortable Corner takes this to the next level by combining an attractive food source (the plot) with cover (brush, etc.). The cover is created in the corner where the woodlot and the plot meet, which provides the comfort factor. The food serves as an attractant.

To build a Comfortable Corner, you'll likely need to increase sunlight to the corner, and enrich the soil with lime and fertilizer. If you're working with a wooded corner, you'll probably need to remove about two-thirds of the overstory for about 50 yards in all directions. For that reason, be sure to choose your stand-trees first. The chainsaw work will regenerate brush and young trees, and the area will grow up with forbs, briars and other food and cover. Deer tend to stage in this area, and bump around in the brush while browsing before entering the plot. They will also seek this area as the safest way to enter the food plot. This makes an ideal bowhunting site. However, do not be overhunt it. Too much human contact quickly turns the corner from a comfortable corner to a corner to avoid.

How much activity is too much? It's best to hunt such sites, at most, once or twice a week. Get in, get out, and give it plenty of rest. Overhunting eliminates daytime deer utilization. If deer detect your presence, they'll feed nocturnally. On evening hunts, try not to leave your stand when deer are still feeding in the plot. Even if it's dark, have someone pick you up on an ATV, which moves deer off the plot without overly alarming them.

Food Plots for Hunting

Food Plots Should Work Together

Food plots should not be laid out in isolation on your property. That is, they should relate to each other. The accompanying diagram shows about 50 acres of cover and food plots. Notice how the boomerang and hourglass hunting plots relate to the large "destination food plots" and bedding areas. Note

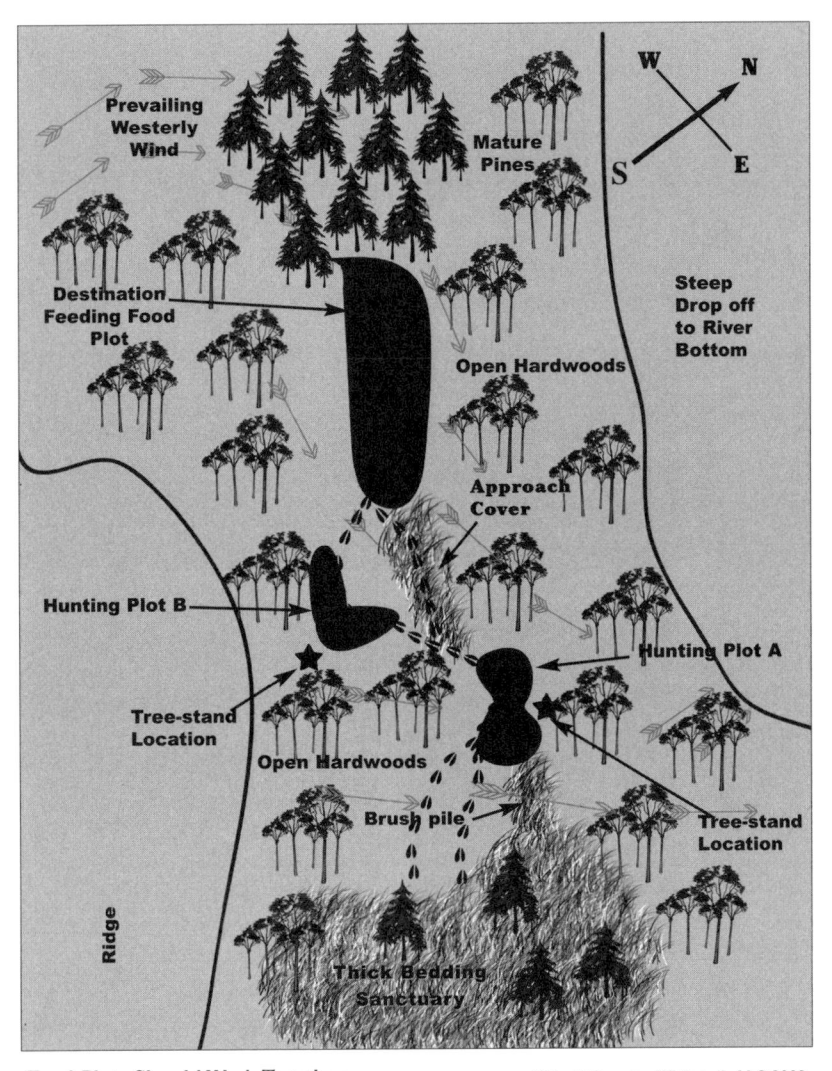

Food Plots Should Work Together ©NorthCountry Whitetails LLC 2002

also how smaller hunting plots relate to each other, and how one works in a north-northwest wind, and the other works in a south-southwest wind. Plan your layouts carefully, both from macro (overall property) and micro (individual plots) levels.

Plantings

While perennials are great for feeding plots, annuals come into their own as hunting plots. We like to plant hunting plots with annuals that are designed to offer peak palatability when we want to hunt over them. We normally plant in mid-August to mid-September. We like BioLogic's Greenpatch Plus — a mix of wheat, oats, clovers and brassicas — for bow season, which runs mid-October to mid-November. And we really love

This 180-class buck was taken in late November 2002 by bowhunter Carl Whittier of Ontario, Canada. The buck was shot on one of Neil's signature plots, the Strip Stake Out, a brassicas plot. It's difficult to tell who is happier, Carl or Neil. Neil helped Carl set up the food plot.

Food Plots for Hunting

This big guy will be in and out of this small hunting plot in no time. During the rut, chances are he won't even stop to eat. Be ready before he shows because you won't get a second chance.

BioLogic's Maximum, which is three or more varieties of brassicas, for early November through the end of hunting season. Clover patches work well at both times, but in our area, they're best planted in spring. It's possible to plant clovers in the fall, but chances are they won't come into their own until the next year. A good stand of brassicas planted in spring also makes a terrific hunting plot come late fall.

Hunting food plots are great places to spend time. We have spent hundreds of hours in and over them, and never tire of the up-close, personal encounters they provide with deer and other wildlife. Lay them out carefully, plant them with cultivars deer prefer during the hunting season, and you'll experience deer hunting like you've never known before.

We promise!

Photo by Charles J. Alsheimer

Chapter XI

Big Toys
for Big Boys (and Girls)

The NorthCountry tram pulls into a large food plot. On your right is a row of well-used farm implements: plows, disks, spreaders, sprayers and a cultipacker. These are the serious tools of the food-plot trade. To your left rests sample bags of lime and fertilizer. A soil-sampling probe leans against the bags, further evidence of serious agricultural practices. Six half-acre test plots stretch before you, including this year's cafeteria-style food plot, where some 75 experimental New Zealand cultivars are being tested. You have entered Biologic's Northern Field Research Center. Ten years before we knew virtually nothing about agricultural practices. In fact, we didn't know a disk from a drag. But thanks to some local farmer friends, we've acquired a solid grasp of what it takes to get the job done. If we can do it, believe us, you can too! This chapter will get you started.

Hunting food plots and small feeding food plots can be created with machines that range from simple hand tools to powerful tractors and plows. The same equipment that farmers use can be effective, but it's not mandatory, especially when you're just starting out. If you have a small area to work or are on a limited budget, you can still create food plots and attractive hunting spots. At its simplest, you can use a rake to rough up bare soil, spread some seed, and stamp it in with your feet. This is as basic as it gets, but it works. There is no smell of fuel fumes, no noisy equipment, and nothing to break — except your back if you do more than a few hundred square feet. This is just pure satisfaction. But if you're like most people, you'll soon graduate to more advanced methods.

ATVs for Small Plot Plantings

The next level of planting sophistication uses more serious equipment and a mechanized power source. This usually means

ATV implements can be handy for planting logging roads and small clearings of one or two acres. The "PlotMaster" is an all-in-one implement that saves time and labor by combining soil preparation, seeding and rolling in one pass. It's a serious piece of equipment.

Big Toys for Big Boys (and Girls)

Unlike some "mini disks," this disk from Monroe Tufline is no toy. It's fabricated out of high-quality heavy-duty steel, and it's made to last like full-sized equipment. This disk will stand up to years of service.

ATV equipment, because most hunters own or can borrow an ATV. A variety of light-duty ATV attachments are available to help habitat managers create small food plots. ATVs are especially effective in remote, hard-to-reach areas or on small hunting plots like Neil's "Boomerang Bushwhack," the "See-Through Hourglass," or the "Long Shot S" designs (see previous chapter).

Be careful. Some ATV implements work great, but others are little more than toys. It's important to consider the weight of the implement you're using, especially in tough soils where you need substantial weight to cut into the ground. Backyard garden implements designed to be pulled by a light-duty lawn mower won't cut it. In addition, you need favorable soil conditions. Moist, but not wet, soils work up the best in most areas. Hard, sun-baked soil should be avoided at all costs, because it's almost impossible to work. We've had great success with Monroe Tufline's pull-behind disks and spreaders. They make several models for small tractors and large ATVs that are moderately priced.

We have also used the Plotmaster with much satisfaction. The Plotmaster contains disks, plows, rollers, drags and a seeder. It weighs 600 pounds and it's a solid piece of equipment. It's far better than buying a yard full of implements, and it retails for about $3,000. It's the only ATV implement you'll need for developing small plots.

If you have a 400cc or larger four-wheel-drive ATV, you can get a lot of work done, but it's unrealistic to expect to plant 4- and 5-

Although we own a 250-gallon sprayer with a 40-foot boom, we usually use this ATV sprayer by Monroe Tufline. Its 25 gallon capacity will treat about one acre with herbicide or pesticides, but it's value is its versatility and maneuverability. It's easy to maneuver in and out of tight spots, and transportation is a snap.

Big Toys for Big Boys (and Girls)

acre fields with ATV implements. The amount of time required to get the job done is much too great. Logging roads and ½- to 1-acre fields can be planted with ease with the PlotMaster and other high-quality ATV implements.

You might also consider a heavy-duty pull-behind mower if you have an ATV. Mowing brush and overgrown fields is an important part of creating habitat. ATV pull-behinds generally have their own gasoline engines. These mowers won't handle heavy brush, but they will cut trails and clearings in the weeds.

This handy 50-hp tractor is about right for serious food-plot planting. It handles a two-bottom plow with ease, and doesn't even groan when pulling 12-foot cultipackers and disks. A bucket is super handy and well-worth the extra cost.

If you're expecting to plant large feeding food plots, you'll need a variety of farm implements. For most situations, a 35- to 60-hp tractor is sufficient. You will also need a set of plows to go with the tractor. In fact, when preparing light soil or worked soil, a disk is often sufficient, and you won't need a plow. If you're shopping for plows, the rule of thumb is one bottom of plow for every 20 horsepower of tractor. Bottoms are the paddles that cut into the ground. After purchasing plows, you'll need a disk, a cultipacker or roller, and some way to spread seed. You'll also need a way to

This John Deere Gator has been the workhorse of our operation. We use it daily for dozens of projects, including seeding, hauling fertilizer and lime, cutting wood and, yes, transporting deer.

spray herbicide and, occasionally, pesticide. We have found the most practical way to spray Roundup® is with a small 25-gallon sprayer made for an ATV. About 25 gallons of fluid — one tank — will spray one acre. Although we have a 200-gallon tractor pull-behind commercial sprayer, we usually use the small four-wheeler model, because it's easier to handle.

Most of this equipment can be bought at auctions. The approximate costs are as follows: tractor, $2,000 to $6,000; plows, two or three bottom set, $275; an 8-foot disk, $525; 10-foot cultipacker, $650; a new sprayer (order through Cabela's or Bass Pro Shops), $150.

The herbicides Roundup® and Poast® can be very effective in saving time and controlling unwanted vegetation. We didn't

Big Toys for Big Boys (and Girls)

use herbicides the first few years we had food plots. Previously, the process was to plow a field over, wait four or five days until the root systems and vegetation began to show again, then disk the field, leveling the plowed ground. We would then wait two weeks for any living plants to regenerate and shoot back up. Then we would again disk and eliminate most of these weeds. All the time, we were using expensive fuel and compacting our already dense clay soil below while pulverizing the top few inches.

We would have a relatively weed-free food plot for a year or so until weeds and grasses appeared again. By the second year we were mowing the plots to eliminate weeds. By the third or fourth year, we were about ready to start over again. That was just too much time and work for weekend warriors who had to travel 2$^1/_2$ hours to work their property. Using herbicides cuts the time

This 100-hp 4WD beauty is a bit of overkill for most food-plot work. Neil uses it in large feeding plots, where it makes quick work of any project, but we could get by without it. This is truly a big toy for big boys (and girls).

dramatically, saves fuel, and avoids excessive soil compaction in clay-type soils. It also keeps weeds in check much longer.

During the late 1990s, we learned we could spray Roundup® one weekend — which took perhaps one hour — and then plow the food plot the next weekend, disk the next day, and then seed and plant. This amounted to two weekends worth of work and about three hours per acre. We spent only six hours per acre with the old method, but it dragged on for weeks. Because our property is located at a high elevation in the North, we must take advantage of spring soil moisture. As soon as the ground is ready to work, we need to get our seeds into the ground to get the most

• •

With proper management and the selective use of herbicides, we have extended the life of our food plots to six years or more.

• •

out of our relatively short growing season. Using herbicide allows us to seed earlier and take advantage of ideal planting conditions. With multiple food plots and limited time, we can't afford to drag out the work over an extended period.

After establishing a plot by starting with a herbicide kill, we do not see many weeds showing up until three or four years later. When grass begins to invade our plots, we use another herbicide, Poast®, which eliminates grass, but does not kill broadleaf cultivars like chicory, brassicas and clover. Poast® keeps out the invading grasses and lets our broadleaf cultivars thrive. With proper management and the selective use of herbicides, we have extended the life of our food plots to six years or more. In fact, according to Dr. Grant Woods, we have the oldest existing

Biologic Premium Perennial plot in the country. This is not to say we're crazy about herbicides. We only use them when necessary, which usually means one application per year. But we have evolved from abstaining skeptics to cautious believers. As a management tool, herbicides are effective and should be considered.

Another advantage of herbicides is that they allow you to practice "no-till" farming. When establishing new plots, no-till is highly recommended. In no-till agriculture, you skip the plowing and disking, and go straight to the seeding. No-till seeders cut nar-

• •

One or two passes with an 8- or 10-foot wide rototiller will generally prepare even the nastiest food plot for seeding.

• •

row slits into the ground — or dead thatch that has been treated with herbicide — with a blade-like hook, and deposit seeds into the slit. The slit closes automatically, and a week or so later green growth pops up in neat rows in your food plots.

No-till equipment has only one catch. It's very expensive. Because of its effectiveness and its relatively new presence in agriculture, you don't often see used no-till seeders for sale. But if money is no object, or you can hire a farmer who has one, no-till could be the way to go.

Some food-plot enthusiasts have great success with heavy-duty rototillers behind their tractors. Once again, these are not the toys you see in backyard gardens. They're serious, heavy-duty implements carrying serious price tags.

One or two passes with an 8- or 10-foot wide rototiller will generally prepare even the nastiest food-plot for seeding. However, large rocks can wreak havoc with a rototiller, so if your soil has more rocks than dirt, find another alternative.

No-till seed mixtures are rarely a good choice. We wish we didn't have to write this chapter and that you could wave the magic food-plot wand and have perfect plots every time. The reality of the food-plot business is that you'll need mechanized equipment to get the job done. In our experience, no-till mixtures only work when perfect conditions exist, which is almost never.

• •

Throwing expensive seed atop unprepared ground is like throwing your hard-earned money onto the same ground and just walking away.

• •

We suggest you think through your equipment needs and seek the advice of an experienced farmer about what works best on your soil. Throwing expensive seed atop unprepared ground is like throwing your hard-earned money onto the same ground and just walking away.

Auctions and Roadside Sales

Unless you're smart about equipment, you must be careful at auctions. Fixing broken equipment is expensive and time-consuming. If you don't know what you're looking at, take an equipment expert with you. He will know what he's looking at and how much to pay. We've bought a few bargain pieces of equipment at

Big Toys for Big Boys (and Girls)

roadside sales that have turned into overgrown rabbit shelters riddled with broken and twisted pieces of steel.

A good friend of ours gave a retired farmer friend an equipment wish list, a budget and a checkbook. The retired gentleman is happy to visit local auctions — and all farmers like auctions — because he has a goal and money to spend. This man knows his equipment and spends our friend's money like it's his own.

Whatever you do, don't buy junk. You need serviceable equipment. Junk equipment wastes your valuable time and money. You'll turn wrenches instead of planting, and worse, junky equipment can kill you. Early in our "farming career," Craig almost bought the farm when the brakes on an old bargain tractor let go, and he headed backward down a steep incline. He escaped injury, but the scare was incredible. Two weeks later, a 50-hp trac-

Used equipment usually requires new owners to be handy with a wrench. Regular maintenance is a must with older equipment. Better to fix it in the shed than break it in the field.

tor with almost-new shiny green and yellow paint replaced the death-trap. The newer tractor had given us perfect service for the 10 years leading up to this book.

Of course, no serious operation is complete without a PTO-driven rotary mower, also known as a brush-hog. These mowers vary from 5 feet wide to double batwings that can mow more than 20 feet of brush at a time. You must match your mower to your tractor, however, because too much PTO horsepower destroys a mower. Conversely, too much mower can damage your tractor. In general, a 6- to 7-foot mower matches up pretty well with a 30- to 50-hp tractor.

You can do tremendous amounts of habitat work with a rotary mower. Overly mature brush is made fresh again by mowing.

Try to buy serviceable, reliable equipment when buying used machinery. Spending a weekend working on a tractor instead of planting is a terrible use of your time. All but the wealthiest food-plot enthusiast will purchase used equipment. Keep it well maintained, and don't buy junk!

Big Toys for Big Boys (and Girls)

Nasty, abandoned fields can be turned into deer feeding areas with mowing, liming, and a good dose of fertilizer. Lanes can be cut, and edge cover can be created with a routine mowing program. We mow brushy areas to ensure they're producing fresh cover and to keep them from maturing to the point where the overstory eliminates food and ground cover. Indeed, next to a chainsaw, a good rotary mower might be one of your most important purchases.

A well-equipped deer hunting property is generally a well-run operation. Although getting started is sometimes difficult, once you get on top of the equipment curve, it's relatively easy to stay there. Add equipment as your budget allows, and as your habitat-development program grows. Running good equipment can be fun. Working on broken junk all weekend when you should be planting is one of the most frustrating parts of habitat development. It drains energy and prevents you from achieving your goals. Regular maintenance of good, serviceable equipment helps you avoid this situation as much as possible.

Photo by Charles J. Alsheimer

Chapter XII

Selecting Cultivars for the Food Plot

You jump off the NorthCountry tram and find yourself thigh-high in a three-tiered food plot. The top tier is filled by broadleaf brassicas plants, which look like broccoli leaves and smell like cabbage. At the next level, you see chicory, a dandelion look-a-like, only much larger. Close to the ground are four varieties of clover, each at a different stage of growth and maturity. This plot is a virtual salad bar for whitetails. Your tour leader asks you to pick a plant and taste it. You taste one and then another. The first plant is much less bitter than the second. You notice deer have grazed the first variety heavily. The lights start going on for you, just as they did for us when Dr. Grant Woods got us tasting food-plot forage three years before. Before that introduction to taste tests, we knew little about peak palatability, whitetail nutrition and selecting forages.

A cultivar is a species planted for a specific purpose. In our case, the purpose is deer food. A "blend" is a number of cultivars planted together in a plot to provide variety.

Photo by Charles J. Alsheimer

Food plots remain important year-round. This lactating doe and her fawn need all of the spring/summer nutrition they can get. Getting this young buck off to a good start pays dividends in the months and years that follow.

When selecting cultivars for food plots, it's important to ask the question: "What do I want my food plots to contribute to the overall management program?" Do you just want something green to hunt over? If so, an annual cultivar planted during fall is usually green for hunting season and attracts deer. It won't be around next spring, but it will feed deer from late summer through fall. You might want to try BioLogic's Green Patch — a mixture of oats, wheat, clovers and brassicas — or Fall Attractant — a mixture of brassicas. Or, do you want cultivars that feed deer year-round, nourish lactating does and their fawns, and put pounds and antler inches on bucks? If so, you'll want a perennial food plot, which in the North is usually planted in spring, lasts four to five years, and produces highly nutritious forage from spring through fall. Biologic's Clover Plus, a mixture of clovers and chicory, is ideal.

Selecting Cultivars for the Food Plot

Or, you might want a year-round, high-protein food supply with a special late-season food source to help carry deer over the winter. In this case, choose a mixture of annual and perennial plants such as like Biologic's Premium Perennial. This is a mixture of

Many clovers shoot up quickly in early spring. By June they're knee high or taller. We call these "feel-good" clovers because you feel good when you see them growing. Unfortunately, they're not the best for deer.

brassicas, clovers and chicory. The clovers and chicory deliver the "groceries" in spring, summer and fall, with the brassicas getting heavily eaten in fall and winter.

It's important to understand that different plantings bring different performance traits to your food-plot program. Study cultivar options to understand how they perform in the field, and what they bring to your deer's table. Don't settle for an "if it's green it's good" food-plot philosophy. You can do better than that.

We believe the goal of a serious Northern food plot is to feed deer with high-quality forage for as many months as possible during the year. This is most readily achieved by planting a variety of cultivars with different growth characteristics, maturation times, and palatability peaks. Some plants do well in dry conditions, others need more moisture, and others do better in the cold. Still others require warm weather. We like to plant a virtual salad bar of highly nutritious cultivars. Multiple cultivars allow us to meet several nutritional needs through a full range of growing conditions.

Feed Palatability

You also must know when cultivars offer peak palatability to effectively use them. Peak palatability means when a cultivar is most attractive to deer. In our area, palatability changes are most noticeable with brassicas. Deer feed little on brassicas until the plant experiences a hard freeze. After such a freeze, it's as if someone threw the feeding switch. Deer go from a nip here and there to a brassicas "mow-down."

We see a more subtle example during late spring and summer in plots containing a mixture of clovers and chicories. If you get down on your hands and knees and look closely, you'll see how deer repeatedly nip the same variety of clover or chicory. They'll ignore dozens of other clovers or chicories growing an inch or two nearby. This is peak palatability. Deer key on individual cultivars at specific times in the cultivars' growth cycle.

This phenomenon is obvious on our "cafeteria test" at the Demo Center. We plant 150 of our 10- x 10-foot test squares with 75 different seeds. Each seed variety is planted in two separate squares. In all, the squares cover a half-acre. The deer can feed cafeteria style in any square they choose. Time after time, we see deer selecting the same two squares in the grid of 150. It's clear they have strong preferences for certain cultivars at specific times.

It's important to understand this concept and plant hunting plots according to each plant's peak palatability. Alfalfa is a good example. In our area, alfalfa loses its appeal after a freeze. Deer forsake it overnight. It makes little sense to plant a late-season hunting plot in alfalfa. On the other hand, brassicas is very attractive after a hard freeze. That's the cultivar we want in a late-season hunting plot.

Selecting Cultivars for the Food Plot

A handful of (red) cattle clover vs. a handful of deer-forage clover (3 white, 1 red). The differences are obvious. The stemmy, lignin-heavy clover on top grows tall and straight for harvest and storage. The clover blend below has fine, delicate stems and would be almost impossible to dry and bale. Different clovers serve different purposes.

Avoid Cattle Forages

When considering food-plot plantings, distinguish between cattle forage and deer forage. Our country has been producing commodity cattle for hundreds of years. As a result, virtually all feeds available at seed stores are designed to be eaten by cattle. The research driving the development of cattle forages sought higher yields of milk or beef. The goal was to create crops that could be harvested and stored in a barn for winter feeding as dry material. That's why most cattle forages are so stemmy. It's easier to harvest, dry and bale high-standing stemmy forages.

Recently, however, new blends were developed specifically for deer consumption. The best blends are produced in New Zealand, where raising deer is as important as raising sheep and cattle. Deer farmers in New Zealand have experimented with deer forages for decades, and are creating food-plot blends containing higher percentages of usable protein than cattle products. The research driving the development of deer forages is designed to produce better venison and antlers, not milk and beef. The forages were developed to be grazed in fields, not harvested and stored inside barns. Many of these cultivars are incorporated into Mossy Oak Biologic's food-plot blends. We've had excellent success with Biologic seed blends. In fact, Biologic experimental blends are regularly tested at the NorthCountry Demo Center for growth characteristics and preference.

Clovers are the Key

Clover blends are the workhorse plants for most food plots. They can contain about 25 percent protein. Clovers grow during spring, summer and into fall. If you plan to plant a clover plot, you want mixtures of clovers engineered for consumption by whitetailed deer. Many clovers shoot up quickly in early spring. By June, they're knee-high or taller. We call these "feel-good" clovers, because you feel good when you see them. Unfortunately, they're not the best for deer. They have a lot of stem material, but not as much succulent, high-protein leafy material. These clovers were developed to be harvested and fed dry to cattle.

Unfortunately, deer don't digest stems well. Stems are high in lignin, which makes stems rigid, and deer digest lignin inefficiently. Cattle, however, digest lignin easily. As a result, most alfalfas and tall stem clovers are best suited to cattle. We like thin-stemmed New Zealand clovers that grow dense and low to the ground. They're designed for deer consumption in the wild, not for dry feed for barnyard cows. Blended clovers mature at different times and are selectively eaten by picky deer. Low, dense clovers also smother

Selecting Cultivars for the Food Plot

This buck was taken on a field planted with BioLogic's Green Patch Plus. This planting is great for fall food plots, featuring oats, wheat, clovers and some brassicas thrown in for good measure. It's truly a blend for any and all autumn conditions.

weeds and grasses better than high, stemmy clovers, which is a plus when trying to get multiple years out of food plots.

Clovers should be planted as blends. Almost any clover will do well in spring, but a well-blended clover plot should perform well year-round under all but the most extreme conditions. You achieve this type of performance by using clovers with diverse characteristics, including maturation rate, heat and drought tolerance, cold-weather performance characteristics, and, of course, tolerance to grazing. It sounds complicated and, frankly, it is. Developing seed blends is an art best left to the pros. Most high-quality premium forage blends are developed to provide food-plot diversity. We, of course, have had great luck with the BioLogic blends.

This NorthCountry client proudly examines the high-quality chicory and brassicas he grew the first year he planted BioLogic's Premium Perennial. This 5-acre field produces more than 50 tons of high-quality winter forage.

Chicory: A Well-Kept Secret

The goal of a hard-working food plot is to cover all weather and growing conditions while providing nutrition and palatability. We're going to put a lot of time, money and energy into the food plot. We don't skimp on seed blends. As a hedge against Mother Nature, we always use clover mixes with chicory, which looks like a dandelion. Chicory is about 22 percent protein, and has a long taproot that's excellent for droughts and hot weather. It's also efficient at transferring minerals from soils to deer. We like it much better than alfalfa, which is also drought-resistant, because it doesn't have a woody stem like alfalfa. It's also much, much easier to grow. In a recent drought year at the Demo Center, we went 45 days without rain. Most clover varieties turned brown and dormant. The chicory thrived as if no amount of heat or drought could stress it. Deer stayed on the plots, working the chicory day after day. With a chicory blend, you're pretty well covered through the dry, hot summer periods.

Brassicas: Secret Weapon of the North

Northern deer managers need to plant with heavy frost and cold, freezing temperatures in mind. Biologic's brassicas plants are rape-like cultivars from New Zealand, and are superior cold-weather forages. When planted in early spring, brassicas achieve maximum — knee- to thigh-high — growth by fall. This, of course, depends on soil conditions and moisture.

In very good growing conditions, brassicas can grow waist high. The plant is 34 percent to 38 percent crude protein, and is

After the entire providence of Ontario turned winter brown, bowhunter Carl Whitier's food plots were still green with brassicas. It's little wonder deer flocked to them from miles around.

mostly leaves. Brassicas has a bitter taste when it first comes up, but works well when planted with other forages. Deer use the clover and chicory until brassicas sweetens. If you taste it in midsummer, it still isn't sweet enough for a salad. After a killing frost, a chemical change occurs, creating sugars. Deer seem to go nuts over brassicas just when our clover and chicory approach dormancy. It's perfect timing. The waist-high, high-protein brassicas plants provide nutrition and attract deer throughout the hunting season and beyond. With a brassicas planting, you can grow up to 10 tons of forage in just one acre when deer — especially big bucks — need it most: after the rut. We've found that brassicas plants stay green and upright in cold weather until consumed by deer, or until they break down in spring.

Brassicas becomes highly attractive to Northern deer after a hard frost, snow or freeze. This buck prefers clover and chicory all spring and summer, but is drawn to brassicas during winter.

Selecting Cultivars for the Food Plot

Deer paw through the snow and feed heavily on brassicas from November through early March. Our best late-season hunting plots are brassicas-based. Spring green-up occurs in early April in our region. Unfortunately, it's an annual plant and must be replanted each spring. But that's easy. You simply cast new brassicas seed — BioLogic's "Maximum" is five or six varieties of brassicas — on top of your plot while the clover and chicory are dormant or just waking up. Brassicas makes its way through the other cultivars to contact the earth and germinate. It will be ready by late summer. Brassicas, when combined with clover and chicory, creates a great three-tiered smorgasbord. Biologic markets several

> *As deer managers, we must be concerned with the herd's overall health. In the North, brassicas is often the only green source of high-protein forage during the later hunting season and beyond.*

food-plot blends that feature assorted brassicas plants. Our favorite is Biologic's Premium Perennial, because it also contains clovers and chicory.

As deer managers, we must be concerned with the herd's overall health. In the North, brassicas is often the only green source of high-protein forage during the late hunting season and beyond. Alfalfa is already brown and dormant, while standing corn and rye are low-protein foods. Brassicas will be used in bow season and gun season, and on through January, February and into March when all but the browse forages are gone.

By December, mature bucks might have lost 25 percent of their body weight because of rutting activity. With a healthy winter supply of brassicas in your food plots, you'll provide deer a

Photo by Charles J. Alsheimer

These post-rut bucks are getting a heavy dose of protein just when they need it most. This brassicas plot helps them recover weight they lost during the rut. Next spring they will convert food into antlers rather than replacing lost weight.

prime food source to regain weight. This ensures you'll retain those bucks for the following season. You don't want to find them piled up in March snowbanks. Also, a good winter and early spring diet allows a buck to enter the antler-growing season in prime condition and put most of his nutrition into growing massive racks. Biologic Premium Perennial has the right ratio of brassicas seed, clover and chicory to ensure you have a good stand of plants. We've had great luck with it.

In the first 10 years we owned the land now occupied by the research facility, we never saw deer wintering on the highest elevations of our property, which is 2,200 feet. No matter the habitat quality we created, deer always left the high ground for sheltered valleys and south-facing slopes. In those 10 years, we recovered only three shed antlers from more than 500 acres, even though we

Selecting Cultivars for the Food Plot

combed the property each spring. The deer just left the property. It was that simple.

The first year we tried Biologic Premium Perennial, we checked the property in late January. With 24 inches of snow on the ground, we had to use a snowmobile to reach the Biologic test plot. To our amazement, we found deer tracks and droppings everywhere. The following spring, we recovered a 2½-year-old's shed in the middle of our 1-acre test plot. The next summer we increased the test plot to three acres of Biologic Premium Perennial and eagerly waited for winter to see what would happen. The following January, again on a snowmobile, we found the plot littered with tracks and signs of deer pawing through 12 inches of snow to reach the still-green brassicas. When spring arrived, we found three sheds in the field. We now plant as much Premium Perennial and brassicas as possible to nourish deer and give them premium food during winter.

One March afternoon, four years after the original planting of our 3-acre plot, we found nine sheds lying there. These antlers were from seven different 1½-year-old bucks that spent winter on our property. Those guys soon became shooters. In spite of the severe weather at this elevation, deer hang around because the food source is beneficial. If chicory is our summer secret weapon, brassicas is our winter wonder. We can't recommend brassicas enough for cold-weather deer diets. We now find high-quality sheds in almost all of our food plots.

Inoculation: A Shot in the Arm for Seeds

Cultivars such as clovers, alfalfa and beans are called legumes, and they have a special, amazing capability. They're able to create their own nitrogen. Legumes draw nitrogen from the air and turn it into a usable nutrient for the plant itself. This process is called nitrogen fixation, and occurs in nodules that form on plant roots when they encounter certain bacteria in the soil.

Scientists have learned that exposing, or inoculating, raw seed to this plant-specific bacteria increases the germination rate and creates stronger, denser stands of young cultivars. Practitioners, especially weekend food-plot warriors, know that inoculating seed is a royal pain. It's a messy, imperfect process if you don't know what you're doing. For starters, it seems you never can find the right inoculant for the legume you're planting, and when you do locate the right one, you must buy enough to do 100 pounds of seed at a time. Then you must mix it into a slurry and blend it with seed. Once you open your bag of inoculant, it begins to die. In fact, some bacteria are dead within a few hours of being exposed to air. This is especially true if they're left in sunlight or heat. They're difficult to store, and are a handful for most people.

What's a fellow to do? Science makes it possible to coat legume seeds with an inoculant and then encapsulate the active seed in a protective layer of hard lime. It's kind of like an M&M candy, where the peanut is the legume seed, the chocolate is the inoculant, and the bright melt-proof sweet coating is the lime.

Almost all high-quality food-plot forage seeds — at least the legumes — are pre-inoculated by manufacturers. Always look for inoculated seed when buying food-plot blends. If you can find inoculated seed that is encapsulated in a protective layer of lime, so much the better. Always check expiration dates, because even encapsulated inoculants lose their effectiveness in a few years.

This mother's milk for seedlings will jump-start your tiny plants and ensure their careers as nitrogen fixers get a good start. Don't waste your money on low-cost seed that has not been inoculated. Without inoculant, seeds don't do well and, frankly, it's too much hassle to inoculate seeds yourself.

Plant Grains to Start a Plot

On areas with marginal soils — i.e., pH in the low 5s — we might not be able to grow premium food-plot products until the lime starts to kick in and we raise the pH. In these instances, we like BioLogic's Green Patch, which can produce a good annual food plot in autumn, and is economical to plant. It will probably be green the following early spring and draw some deer, but it will soon be abandoned for more preferred cultivars. It's an excellent attractant blend and a great "place-holder" until you can get your soil ready for higher-dollar premium blends. This is also true for rye, grain, oats and winter wheat, but we prefer a blend over a straight planting of grain forages.

Corn: Just Say No

Many people want to plant corn in food plots. We call corn a one-month wonder in areas with a high deer population. Therefore, we don't plant corn for deer. The young, green corn plant does nothing for lactating does or antler-growing bucks during spring and summer. In fact, if nipped as a young plant, corn will usually fail to grow ears. When it's ready for eating in autumn, it only provides cover and 8 percent protein, at best. In highly populated areas, if corn makes it through the shoot stage, deer will eat the tassel and silk, thus eliminating its ability to grow ears. With corn, your ground is tied up from spring until fall, and all for just a one- or two-week feeding frenzy in August or September. When deer need nutrition most, the ground is brown dirt. It's much better to take that 1-acre food plot and try to grow a perennial clover and chicory mix to maximize food benefits for deer.

We want to see edible green as early in spring as possible. Corn is an excellent energy and high-carbohydrate source, but it's relatively weak in protein. Its principal value comes as a fall attractant, but the same is true of some rich, green plots that nourish deer year-round. To make matters worse, farmers plant it by the mile, providing stiff competition. Even so, a good, green food plot in corn country provides the variety whitetails crave. Leave the corn planting up to farmers unless you have acres and acres of food-plot space available for clover- and brassicas-based forage and corn plantings.

Deciding what to plant in food plots can be as easy or difficult as you choose to make it. It is never an exact science and, like all things weather-dependent, Mother Nature has a lot to say about how your plots fare each year.

Whitetails love corn, especially in fall and winter. Unfortunately, corn is a "one-month wonder" in most regions, and ties up valuable soils all spring and summer without contributing anything to a deer's nutritional needs. We prefer plots with cultivars that work year-round.

Selecting Cultivars for the Food Plot

A little research and planning, however, pays huge dividends. Before selecting a cultivar or cultivar blend, think about the role you've chosen for this planting. Are you creating a quarter-acre green patch for a month of bow season, or do you think you'll provide deer some serious year-round tonnage in a 5-acre plot? Also, do you want the planting to last five years or five weeks?

Analyze seed labels and call seed producers' hotlines with questions. Visit the Web sites of companies like NorthCountry Whitetails (www.NorthCountryWhitetials.com) and BioLogic (www.mossyoakbiologic.com). Both companies provide valuable information on selecting cultivars. Be careful with "local seeds" sold at feed-and-seed stores. Chances are, these blends consist of cattle forages.

And finally, don't be afraid to experiment. Try one blend here and another there. Mix and match. Pay attention to the deer and how they respond to your plantings. Above all, have fun. This is not open-heart surgery. Nor is it rocket science. If you make a mistake or two, relax. You're in good company. We all make mistakes. Most importantly, don't give up if you suffer a setback with your plantings. There is always next season, and it will have plenty of moisture. Or at least you can hope it does.

Photo by Charles J. Alsheimer

Chapter XIII

Quality Deer Hunting

Your NorthCountry tram tour of the demo center is complete, but you have one more stop. You open the screen door and enter the Demo Center headquarters. Evidence of the hunt surrounds you. Every set of antlers taken in previous years adorns the walls. There must be 50 sets or more. Placed in order by year taken, the antlers show you the project's progress and success. Spikes, forks, and small 6-pointers represent the first two years. Antlers that score in the 100-class occupy the slots for years three, four and five. Then, the record-book bucks start and continue. An occasional forkhorn or small 6-pointer bears witness to a young hunter's first deer or an old timer's last. Shed antlers hanging on a post tell the same story, from spikes to record-book class bucks. Photos preserve the smiling faces of successful hunters. It's clear that camp "Kindred Spirits" practices Quality Deer Hunting.

Quality Deer Hunting (QDH) is our version of Quality Deer Management (QDM). We emphasize creating a quality hunting experience, which includes seeing and hunting mature deer. We're not convinced we can manage a deer *herd*, because of the

This cabin is the center of hunting activity on the Demo Center. Dubbed "Kindred Spirits," its name portrays the camp's fellowship and sense of family. It's a one-for-all and all-for-one camp, where Quality Deer Hunting is practiced without many hard-core rules and regulations.

size of our property, but we can manage the quality of our deer hunting by how we hunt and what we hunt. At camp Kindred Spirits, we embrace the notion of Quality Deer Hunting. We hope this book helps create a quality deer hunting experience, and supports a philosophy of hunting that increases your enjoyment. In our view, nothing beats seeing wild deer benefiting from the habitat-improvement projects you undertake and complete over the years. Nothing beats the togetherness and bonding that comes through habitat work done with friends, family and loved ones. Nothing beats going to bed at night, muscles aching, knowing that today you were a good steward of the land. This book has shown you how to create habitat. But that's only part of the equation. How do we create our quality deer hunting experience, which is the ultimate payoff?

Quality Deer Hunting

Follow QDM Guidelines

First, we embrace the principles of QDM as advanced by the Quality Deer Management Association. We aggressively harvest does, let young bucks mature, and create favorable habitat and food to sustain a healthy herd. We're active members of the QDMA, and have benefited by attending their meetings and reading their magazine, *Quality Whitetails*. But because of the

• •

In our view, nothing beats seeing wild deer benefiting from the habitat-improvement projects you conceive and complete over the years. Nothing beats the togetherness and bonding that comes through creating habitat with friends, family and loved ones.

• •

limited size of our property, 500 acres, and a few cooperating neighbors, another 400 to 500 acres, we don't believe we're actually managing the deer herd in the true sense of controlling a population. Thus, the term "managing" is a bit self-deceiving. We emphasize "self-deceiving" in an attempt to keep what we're doing in perspective.

We can manage our own hunting experience and do so intently. Our hunting set ups and techniques help keep our deer "to home." We're headed in the right direction, and every year more local hunters "get with the program," but we do not yet have control over enough acres to truly manage the herd. Even so, we take great satisfaction in controlling our hunting experience, and that's vital.

In addition to shooter bucks like this, this hunter will harvest numerous does from this food plot each year.

Harvest Does Heavily

The fundamental principles of QDM include harvesting does to create a better doe-to-buck ratio and keep the population in check. We aggressively harvest does. In our area and probably in yours, the ratio should be two or less does per buck. There is only so much carrying capacity on any property. If our resident population is 90 percent does, it decreases our chances to harvest bucks in general. There will be fewer to hunt. The math is simple.

Another reason to harvest does has to do with reproduction. When fewer does are available to breed, more mature bucks do most of the breeding, passing the better genes into the herd and wrapping up the breeding season in a shorter time. In areas with far too many does per buck, and too many deer in general, the breeding season can last three months or more, because not all does are bred the first time they enter estrus. This forces the 3½- to 5½-year-old bucks to run for 90 days or more as does keep coming into estrus every 28 days until they conceive. During this time, bucks take on little food, and lose body weight just before the onset of winter. This routine runs them into the ground, stresses breeding bucks enormously, and causes more of them to succumb to winter's ravages. Furthermore, does bred during the later breeding seasons drop fawns later in the summer. This leads to smaller fawns as autumn and winter approach, which leads to a higher winter mortality rate on fawns.

We try to keep the deer population in check by aggressively harvesting does. We take all the does that New York state will allow us to legally harvest, as long as we believe the ratio is no less than two or three does per buck. If we ever reach a more favorable ratio, we would probably back off on doe harvests for perhaps one season. We use all the meat we can eat, and often contribute to New York's Venison Donation Coalition program. Each year, dozens of hungry families enjoy high-protein, chemical- and steroid-free venison taken from our property. One deer provides about

These boxes of donated venison create thousands of high-protein meals. Hunters feeding the hungry with donated venison is a great idea and a boon to deer managers who need to harvest does.

160 servings of meat. We encourage hunters everywhere to share their harvest with the needy through one of the excellent venison-donation programs in their area. With deer numbers on the rise and hungry people in every community, it's a win-win situation.

Let Young Bucks Walk

One of our goals has always been to create a more mature buck age structure within the herd by allowing young deer to grow up. Harvesting bucks that are at least 2½ years old ensures you'll have 2-, 3- and occasionally 4- and 5-year-old bucks on the

• •

We don't get so hung up on harvest rules and regulations that it interferes with our hunting enjoyment. If a hunter mistakes a button buck for a doe, there is no chastisement, penalty or disgrace.

• •

property. To identify a 2½-year-old buck, look for an antler spread as wide as the deer's ears. This works in most parts of the country. The key is to learn to age bucks on the hoof. Generally, this is done by evaluating a combination of antler mass, spread and overall deer size. Our 2½-year-old bucks weigh between 160 and 180 pounds on the hoof, but that's a regional index. The visual difference between a 1½- and a 2½-year-old buck is obvious.

Once you start seeing 2½-year-olds and above, you'll recognize differences in body sizes more easily. The more deer you see and compare notes on, the better. Video cameras and motion-triggered cameras will help you age deer in your area.

Quality Deer Hunting

Counting points can be deceptive. With proper nutrition, $1\frac{1}{2}$-year-old bucks often sport 8-point racks or better. We've seen $1\frac{1}{2}$-year-old 10-pointers show up on the meatpole. Like all things, you get better at aging animals with practice. Pay attention and practice, and soon you'll be batting almost 100 percent, at least on bucks age $2\frac{1}{2}$ and older.

We do not, however, get so hung up on harvest rules and regulations that it interferes with our hunting enjoyment. If a hunter mistakes a button buck for a doe, we don't chastise, penalize or disgrace. Even experienced hunters make mistakes. Bill Walters, a sheriff and friend from Pennsylvania, and one of our camp regulars, once mistook a button buck for a $1\frac{1}{2}$- year-old doe. His arrow found its mark, but 30 minutes later he was back at camp,

These two bucks are a couple of years apart. The buck on the left looks nice, but is far from being his companion's equal. Note the differences in body size and antler development. The more you study deer in the wild, the better you become at aging deer on the hoof.

head hung low, his apology well-rehearsed. We couldn't help but laugh at his unnecessary remorse. We told Bill this is not open-heart surgery. We're here to hunt and have a good time. Of course, we teased him, but it was good-natured and only added enjoyment to our hunt. Some clubs and managers overdo the rules. We don't punish honest mistakes, and we don't force anyone to hunt big bucks exclusively.

Young Hunters Get the Green Light

We also encourage young hunters and, for that matter, hunters in their later years, to shoot any deer they choose, including yearling bucks. Research shows young hunters who don't experience success drop out of hunting at an alarming rate. We believe young hunters should harvest a few deer as soon as possible after they start hunting. If those deer are year-

> *We believe young hunters should harvest a few deer as soon as possible after they start hunting. If those deer happen to be yearling bucks, so be it. We want youngsters to embrace hunting whole-heartedly.*

ling bucks, so be it. We want youngsters to embrace hunting whole-heartedly. We will always have yearling bucks to pass up.

The same is true for newcomers. Hunters in their teens and early 20s, and even some in their 30s, get the green light to kill young bucks and — of course — does when hunting with us. That is part of our Quality Deer Hunting formula.

Jessi Cole, age 7, celebrates her first kill. Not only did she experience success at an early age, which is critical to becoming a lifetime hunter, but she helped manage the herd with this doe kill.

Katie, a friend of Neil's, had been interested in archery from the beginning of her friendship with Neil. Over a three-year period, her enthusiasm for bowhunting increased and she developed great shooting skills. One fall she felt she was ready to hunt. Putting camo tape on her pretty target bow was a rite of passage. Tight groups in the McKenzie deer target (with broadheads) showed she was ready for the challenge.

That year Neil religiously accompanied Katie during the bow season, helping her judge distances and enjoy the outdoors through the heightened interest of companionship. He happily forfeited his chance for the Pope & Young bucks he watched all summer to help Katie. A buck or doe equally challenged the young college student, as long as it entered her effective bow range of 20 yards and less.

Late in October, opportunity knocked. While hunting with Neil, Katie spotted a buck that seemed headed her way. Whispering quietly, Neil coached her on when to draw the bow, and then "willed" the buck to stop. When the buck paused broadside at 20 yards, Neil thought she had it, but her arrow flew over its back. Katie had jerked up her head to watch the arrow fly, a common mistake for beginners, causing the miss.

Kindred Spirits is an equal-opportunity camp, and Katie's gender didn't spare her the harassment that accompanies a miss — especially with an eyewitness. Nonetheless, Neil was proud of her. She took our kidding in good spirits and climbed back into the stand the next day. As the season continued, she toughed out cold weather, often without seeing a deer. She fell in love with the sport and reveled in the experience of the hunt. She found bear tracks, watched turkeys parade by, and witnessed bucks chasing does. It was all new for her and exciting for all of us in camp.

Neil and Katie with her first bow-kill. Beginning hunters need to experience success, and so they get the green light on all deer on our property. Selective harvesting can come later.

Finally, another opportunity presented itself. A 3-point yearling, its mind clouded by testosterone, stiff-legged past Katie at 20 yards. This time her arrow flew true and the fat young buck piled up 70 yards away in a stand of red pines. That night in camp everyone was so excited you would have thought someone had shot a Boone-and-Crockett book buck. To us, that's what Quality Deer Hunting is all about. Another hunter had experienced the rites of passage at camp Kindred Spirits. The chances of Katie taking a 2½-plus buck or a more mature doe that year were slim. She needed to start with that young fellow.

We rejoice and celebrate our fellow hunters' success and are not too tough on their failures. We're truly a one-for-all and all-for-one group. In fact, we dubbed our cabin "Kindred Spirits" on the day we broke ground for it. Our only true rule is "no yelling at anyone for any reason." This is a rule taken from Rick Bass' terrific book, *The Deer Pasture*. That's probably the most important rule anyone could have in a deer camp.

Follow the 10 Percent Rule

We also try not to get hung up with antler inches. When setting the bar, we use a 10 percent rule. We talk about antler size in inches so we have a common vocabulary, but our goal is to harvest mature bucks that are in the top 10 percent age structure of deer using our property. We advise you to do the same. It sets a reachable standard, and keeps those of us who live in the real world of marginal soils from judging ourselves against standards set for Iowa, Illinois or Kansas.

Location does not affect the 10 percent rule, nor does the maturity of the deer and your management program. Some areas of the country grow bigger deer because it's easier for them to grow old. Or maybe deer in that area benefit from exceptional nutrition. At our place, a top 10 percent buck will be a 4½-year-old, 140-class buck. That same 4½-year-old buck in Iowa could be 180 to 190 inches. By thinking in terms of the top 10 percent, you can have a trophy challenge no matter where your property is located and how far you're into your program. You should always be proud of harvesting a top 10 percent buck,

• •

Our goal is to harvest mature bucks that are in the top 10 percent age structure of deer on our property. This sets a reachable standard of accomplishment, and keeps those of us who live in the world of marginal soils from judging ourselves against Iowa, Illinois or Kansas standards.

• •

even if he nets no more than 90 or 100 points in antler score. We like this sliding scale with its ever-present realistic challenge.

Every year we seem to raise the bar a little higher. Three years into our program, we were thrilled to harvest a 2½-year-old deer. After 12 years in our program, we raised the bar to 3½- and 4½-year-old bucks. Some day, the top 10 percent bucks on our place might be 5½-year-olds. We have seen bucks on our land with more than 150 inches of antlers. In fact, Craig shot one this size in 2002. Every buck we kill goes on the wall. Katie's 3-pointer is sandwiched between two 2½-year-old bucks, yet it's no less of a trophy than the others. They're all trophies to us.

Our sanctuary concept helped the deer reach maturity. Our high-quality food plots increased their weight and antler mass. Our records show a weight increase of 15 percent in the same

This 150-plus B&C buck was taken by Craig the last day of the 2002 gun season. In doing so, he raised the 10 percent bar a bit higher for the seasons that followed. We went from forks and spikes to this in about six years. That's truly amazing!

age and sex categories, when compared to five years before. Rack sizes increased dramatically. We like to think this is because of our quality habitat and hunting program.

During bow season the first year we owned the property, we saw seven bucks, including one "rack" buck, a 2½-year-old. We shot no deer that year with a bow. During the firearms season, we shot one 3-point buck. We rejoiced over our first buck kill. We had seven hunters. We did not hunt does.

After four years of habitat-development work, we were passing up yearling bucks, and our "shooters" were 2½-year-olds, 100-class bucks and above. We had increased the percentage of 2½-year-old bucks to 25 percent of all antlered deer sighted. After 12 years in our program, we expected to see three bucks per hunter per sit, and it's not uncommon to have four hunters see 15 different bucks, half of which are 2½-year-olds. In 2002, 65 percent of the 68 different bucks we sighted were 2½ years old or better.

Our "shooter bucks" became 3½-year-olds with 125 Pope & Young inches and above. Those are dramatic results, especially for western New York state. Sure, these bucks stray off the property and get shot by neighbors, but interestingly, now that the neighbors know they're likely to see one of "our" bigger deer, they're waiting longer and passing more smaller bucks than ever before. They often wind up "settling" for a doe or two for the freezer. They inadvertently are following the harvest principles of QDM. Happily, some got hooked, joined the QDMA, and now read the magazine and participate in the organization.

Neil took these two bucks on back-to-back evening hunts. The 120 B&C bow buck, shot on the last day of archery season, was followed by the 130 B&C gun buck taken the first day of gun season. Talk about quality hunting!

Even so, we know others are just out there waiting for one of the Doughertys' big ones. We don't get worked up about it. We're just happy more young bucks are growing up in our area. When a neighbor kills one of "our" big bucks, that brings him one step closer to becoming a QDM disciple. Remember one thing when your neighbor kills that trophy you fed and watched all summer: Another will soon be there to take his place.

Quality hunting is about lots of things. It's about sitting on a food plot you created, and seeing does and fawns enjoying 35 percent protein forages, watching young bucks sparring and chasing does, and seeing full-racked yearlings instead of spindly spikes. It's about a well-defined rut with scrapes and rubs, and chasing, snorting and grunting. It's about kinship and friendship, and perhaps most of all, it's about stewardship. It adds a special satisfaction that hunting alone cannot deliver.

But the real rush comes from knowing that a top 10 percent deer is out there, and could step out at any moment. You see his rubs on 6-inch trees and his tracks in the soft earth. Every shift is a duel. You function at heightened awareness, because you know he's out there. He's the one you're after, the one you read about and saw on TV.

This excitement, combined with the camaraderie of friends and family, is how we define Quality Deer Hunting. We encourage you to create your own quality hunting experiences. This kind of hunting requires time, commitment, planning and some investment, but it's more than worth it.

Photo by Mossy Oak BioLogic

Nothing compares to the thrill of harvesting a big buck when hunting with friends. Hunting buddies celebrate and enjoy of a friend's success as much as their own.

Join the Quality Deer Management Association

We also suggest you join the QDMA so you can enjoy its many benefits. Attend the group's meetings and read its magazine, *Quality Whitetails*. You will be encouraged by the success stories of QDMA members, and meet people with management goals similar to your own. It's kind of a support group for people like us.

We state unequivocally that you'll succeed if you follow the principles and practices outlined in this book. You will create better habitat and, ultimately, will have quality deer and Quality Deer Hunting.

If you can persuade your neighbors to follow the same program, everyone will benefit. Quality Deer Hunting is contagious, and even the most skeptical old-timers will come around once they see the proof through success. You owe it to yourself and those you care about most to take a run at it.

Photo by Charles J. Alsheimer

Chapter XIV

Getting Started

The NorthCountry tram and Demo Center are now history. You're at home in your favorite chair. If you're lucky, there is a Labrador at your feet and a fire in the stove. But it matters not. Someday there will be. Close your eyes. Imagine your property as a whitetail haven, everything a Quality Deer Hunting property should be. Maybe it's your special 50 acres, your family's 250 or your club's 3,000. Maybe you don't own property, but someday will. Visualize what you want it to be. Be certain. It can happen. Create the dream tonight. Tomorrow when you wake up, make the commitment, and then start planning. Before you know it, you will be hunting top 10 percent deer and enjoying the finest Quality Deer Hunting of your life.

In the pages that follow, Appendix B contains the "Field Notes" worksheets we use when doing site evaluations with our clients. We went to a workbook format after finding research that indicated clients benefit most when collaboration occurs between the "expert" (us) and the "client" (you). In other words, there should be give-and-take and buy-in by both parties.

Basically, when doing a site evaluation, we spend a day or so on a client's land with them alongside. Instead of leaving and mailing a report — our previous practice — we now insist that our clients take a couple of hours to work through the "Planning Guide and Field Notes" worksheets with us (pg. 231). That way, when we leave, the client has a plan in hand and is ready to get to work. Best of all, he wrote the plan in his own words — but with our guidance — and buys into the program.

We find this approach superior to a mailed report, which arrives at a later date, with some concepts fading from memory. Our clients carry this Planning Guide Field Notes in their pickups and keep everything in their camp. This becomes the bible for their quality deer hunting program.

Take a look at Appendix B. Think about the principles outlined in this book, and consider how they might apply to your piece of paradise. Dare to dream. We have seen the dream become reality in hundreds of cases. It has worked for us and it will work for you. Don't settle for a mediocre experience when Quality Deer Hunting is within your grasp.

As the dream begins to take shape, make sure you take time for a reality check. Answer the five "Quality Deer Hunting through Habitat Management Reality Check" questions found in Appendix A. Be brutally honest with yourself. If you can't answer yes to all of these questions, you need to spend time turning your "No" answers into "Yes" answers.

Once you've passed the reality check, it's time to start a plan of your own. Revisit Appendix B. Be sure to make extra copies —

permission granted by authors — before writing on the one provided, because we guarantee your plans will change over time. Start filling in some of the blanks. This book will be a huge help in developing your own plan. Chances are, you will seek an expert's assistance. If so, Neil accepts a limited number of new clients each year.

We wish you well. May you enjoy the same joys of hunting, fellowship and stewardship we have cherished these past several years. May you, too, become a Kindred Spirit.

Photo by Charles J. Alsheimer

Appendix A

A Reality Check for Quality Deer Hunting Through Habitat Management

Directions: Answer "Yes" or "No" to these questions with brutal honesty. If you answer "No" to even one question, it is best to rethink whether you are ready to undertake Quality Hunting and Habitat Development Programs. Try to change each "No" to a "Yes" before going further.

1. Are you dissatisfied enough with your current deer hunting situation to commit time and money for the next five years to improve the quality of your hunting?

2. Are your hunting partners and family of a like mind, and willing to make similar commitments?

3. Do you now, or will you soon, have enough control over a hunting property through a lease or ownership to control how it is hunted, and will you be able to implement habitat-improvement projects on the property?

4. Do you have enough time, money and/or other assets like farm or logging equipment to support a sustained (minimum of five years) commitment to improving the quality of deer hunting on your property?

5. Do you believe, after reading this book and gathering other informative articles, that you have enough knowledge and resources to undertake a program on your own? Or are you prepared to hire a professional to assist with your management plan, and do you know how to contact one?

If you answered "No" to any of the questions, you must analyze why you answered "No," and assess the likelihood of turning each negative answer into a "Yes." In our experience, one or more "No's" will lead to frustration and failure.

If you have honestly answered "Yes" to all five main questions, you are probably ready to go and will improve the quality of deer hunting on your property. Use the forms provided in Appendix B to develop your plan.

⟶

Appendix B

NorthCountry Whitetails
Hunting and Habitat Development

Planning Guide & Field Notes

NorthCountry Whitetails LLC • P.O. Box 925 •Fairport, NY 14450
585-388-6990 • 877–672–7462 • email: info@NorthCountryWhitetails.com
www.NorthCountryWhitetails.com

Goals

Landowner's Goals: (hunting/wildlife, stewardship, economics, etc.)

_____

_____

_____

Site Overview

Site Map - rough sketch of property, including management zones, landmarks, neighboring properties, etc.)

Description of Property:

_____
_____
_____
_____
_____
_____
_____

Property Strengths:

_____
_____
_____
_____
_____
_____

Property Weaknesses:

_____
_____
_____
_____
_____
_____

Property Management Strategies: (strategies employed to achieve goals)

ZONE DESCRIPTION

Zone _____

Description (Characteristics of Zone)

_____
_____
_____
_____
_____
_____
_____

Sketch zone layout

Recommended Practices: (specific practices to be undertaken):

_____
_____
_____
_____
_____
_____
_____
_____
_____
_____
_____

Management Practices Implementation Schedule

High Priority	Zone(s)	Season of Implementation
_____	_____	_____
_____	_____	_____
_____	_____	_____
_____	_____	_____

Moderate Priority	Zone(s)	Season of Implementation
_____	_____	_____
_____	_____	_____
_____	_____	_____
_____	_____	_____
_____	_____	_____

Leisure Time	Zone(s)	Season of Implementation
_____	_____	_____
_____	_____	_____
_____	_____	_____
_____	_____	_____

Equipment Recommendation

Identify Equipment Required to Implement Plan:

Woods Work
- _____ Chainsaw $_____
- _____ Woods Ax and Wedges $_____
- _____ Protective Chaps $_____
- _____ Ear, Eye, Head Protection $_____
- _____ Lopping Shears $_____
- _____ Power Brush Cutter $_____
- _____ Hand Spreader $_____
- _____ Hand Sprayer $_____
- _____ Rake $_____

Food Plots
- _____ ATV $_____
  - _____ PlotMaster $_____
  - _____ Disk $_____
  - _____ Roller $_____
  - _____ Seeder $_____
  - _____ Pull behind Mower $_____
  - _____ Sprayer $_____
- _____ Tractor $_____
  - _____ Disk $_____
  - _____ Cultipacker/Roller $_____
  - _____ Plow $_____
  - _____ Lime Spreader $_____
  - _____ Seeder $_____
  - _____ Seed Drill $_____
  - _____ Sprayer $_____
  - _____ Roto Tiller $_____

General
- _____ Bulldozer
  - _____ New Purchase $_____
  - _____ Used Purchase $_____
  - _____ Rental $_____
- _____ Tractor $_____
  - _____ Rotary Mower (Bushhog) $_____
  - _____ Tractor Bucket $_____

Food Plot Recommendations

Describe Food Plot Location, Design, and Identify Forages Planted:

Plot 1:   Zone ____   pH ____   Lime _____   Fert _____

_____
_____
_____
_____

Plot 2:   Zone ____   pH ____   Lime _____   Fert _____

_____
_____
_____
_____

Plot 3:   Zone ____   pH ____   Lime _____   Fert _____

_____
_____
_____
_____

Plot 4:   Zone ____   pH ____   Lime _____   Fert _____

_____
_____
_____
_____

Confidential Annual Budget
(For Landowner Planning Purposes Only)

	Year 1	Year 2	Year 3
Food Plot			
Liming	$_____	$_____	$_____
Fertilizer	$_____	$_____	$_____
Seed	$_____	$_____	$_____
Labor	$_____	$_____	$_____
Woods Work			
Labor	$_____	$_____	$_____
Road & Trail Building	$_____	$_____	$_____
Security	$_____	$_____	$_____
Equipment			
Purchase	$_____	$_____	$_____
Maintenance	$_____	$_____	$_____
Mowing	$_____	$_____	$_____
Other			
_____	$_____	$_____	$_____
_____	$_____	$_____	$_____
_____	$_____	$_____	$_____
_____	$_____	$_____	$_____
_____	$_____	$_____	$_____
_____	$_____	$_____	$_____
Total	$_____	$_____	$_____

Time Management Requirements

Guidlelines   **Time Requirements**

	Year 1	Year 2	Year 3
Food Plot			
Spring	_____	_____	_____
Fall	_____	_____	_____
_____			
_____			
_____			
Woods Work	_____	_____	_____
_____			
_____			
_____			
Security	_____	_____	_____
_____			
_____			
_____			
Mowing	_____	_____	_____
_____			
_____			
_____			
Road & Trail Building	_____	_____	_____
_____			
_____			
_____			
Equipment Maintenance	_____	_____	_____
_____			
_____			
_____			
Other			
_____	_____	_____	_____
_____	_____	_____	_____
_____	_____	_____	_____
_____	_____	_____	_____
_____	_____	_____	_____
Total	_____	_____	_____

Producing Quality Deer and Quality Hunters

Many hunters are seeking reliable information and proven management techniques to maximize the quality of their deer herds. Whether it's questions about food plots, herd management, or antler growth, the Quality Deer Management Association has the answers from the nation's leading whitetail experts. Call today for more information or to learn how you can join the nation's fastest growing and most respected, non-profit whitetail organization.

www.QDMA.com • 800-209-3337

Index

A

Access 39, 43, 67-68, 71-82, 85, 87, 166
Access Roads 43, 71, 82-83, 101, 124, 136-137
Alfalfa 145, 169, 192, 194, 196, 199, 201
Alsheimer, Charles 19, 20, 22-24, 54, 55, 58, 66
Apple Tree 31, 32, 41, 45, 49, 50, 51, 58, 61, 119, 120
ATV 33, 44, 84, 89-93, 136-137, 143, 170, 176-179
ATV Seeder 143, 176

B

Bio-Logic 15, 20, 21, 33, 139, 145-146, 172, 173, 183, 190, 191, 194, 195, 197, 199, 200, 201, 205
  Clover Plus 95, 98, 190
  Fall Attractant 190
  Green Patch Plus 172, 190, 203
  Maximum 173, 199
  Premium Perennial 91, 183, 191, 195, 196, 199-201
BioLogic Northern Research Facility 175
Birds Foot Trefoil 95
Boundaries 39, 47, 72-73, 75, 82, 103, 107, 109
Bowhunting 13, 17, 22-23, 92, 159, 160, 162-164, 170, 172, 199, 205, 215
Brassicas 18, 20, 133, 138, 145, 147-148, 151, 162, 163, 169, 172, 173, 189, 190-192, 195, 197-201, 204

Briars and Berries 51, 64, 87, 140, 170
Browse 40 46, 51, 53-56, 59-60, 62, 64, 87, 83-95, 108, 111, 114-115, 123, 133, 144, 170, 199
Browse-cut 40-42, 52, 53, 60-64, 93, 94, 111, 113, 126
Buckley, Dave and Beth 21, 22, 39, 114
Bushnell 143

C

Cafeteria Test 175, 192
Chainsaw 31, 41, 42, 46, 49, 51, 52, 57, 59, 64, 65, 115-121, 128, 154, 157, 170, 187
  Safety 115-118, 121
  Safety Gear 46, 65, 116
  Safety Rules 117
Chicory 87, 133, 137-139, 144-147, 162, 189-192, 195-201, 203
Clearcut 17, 57, 60
Clover 14, 40, 43, 64, 87, 88, 92-95, 97, 137, 139, 144-147, 151, 162, 163, 172, 173, 189-191, 193, 194, 196, 198-201, 203, 204
Consulting Forester 125-126
Corn 145, 199, 203, 204
Cover 39-41, 49-50,, 57-59, 64, 87, 94, 104-105, 111, 113, 115, 124-125, 151, 152, 155, 161, 163, 166-171, 187
  Holding Cover 42
Cultivar 173, 175, 182, 189-205

Index

D

Deer Hunting Properties 35, 43, 187
Demo Center 15, 18-19, 22, 24-28, 37, 43, 52, 62, 85, 89, 94, 99, 101, 113, 118-119, 123, 136, 145-147, 192, 194, 207, 208, 225
Denying Access 68
Digestibility 136, 194

E

Entering a Sanctuary 105-107
Equipment
  Bulldozer 44, 96, 128, 130, 153, 154, 157, 158, 161
  Buying 175-186
  Cultipacker 141, 144, 175, 179, 180
  Disk 33, 92, 97, 141, 175, 178, 179, 181-183
  Rotary Mower 158, 161, 186, 187
  Rototillers 183, 184
  Spreader 90-91, 137, 142, 175, 178
  Tractor 33, 61, 65, 81, 82, 90, 91, 120, 124, 138, 138, 144

F

Fertilizer 17, 33, 43, 46, 64, 83, 91, 92, 94, 97, 118-120, 134, 136, 138-140, 170, 175, 187
Food Plots 14, 15, 17-20, 31, 33, 43, 56, 63, 82-83, 91, 92, 96, 98-99, 103, 106, 108, 120, 135, 137, 142, 144-148, 153, 155-159, 161, 163-173, 175-178, 181-184, 189-191, 193-195, 202-204, 218, 221
Food Plot Construction 138-144, 151-173, 175-184
  Feeding Food Plots 133-138, 151, 155, 156, 172, 179, 181
  Food Plots for Hunting 151-153, 156, 157, 159-173, 175, 177, 192, 199
  Neil's Signature Plots 162-170
    Boomerang Bushwhack 163-164, 171, 177
    Comfortable Corner Plot 169-170
    Corner Converger Plot 168-169
    Long Shot S Plot 164-166, 177
    See Through Hourglass Plot 161-164, 171, 177
    Strip Stake Out Plot 166-167
Forages 20, 21, 33, 42, 87, 88, 90-95, 98, 99, 130, 133, 138, 141, 145-146, 158, 162, 166-196, 189-195, 197-199, 203, 204, 221
Forbs 64, 87, 170
Forester 113-114, 125-126, 129
Foulkrod, Bob 22-24
Frost Seeding 97-98

G

Gates 67, 69-71
Grasses 52, 64, 137-138, 140, 181, 195
Ground Blinds 156

H

Habitat Development 15, 19, 23, 25-29, 32, 34-35, 45, 47, 65, 82, 108, 187, 229, 230
Habitat Management 25, 29, 35, 37-38, 41, 123, 226
Hang Ons 155
Herbicide 137-141, 178, 180-183
  Poast® 137-138, 176, 178, 179
  Round Up® 180, 182

I

Inoculating 201, 202

J

John Deere Gator 84, 144, 180

K

Kindred Spirits 207, 208, 216, 217, 227

L

Land
- Finding 34
- Government Programs 35
- Group owning 36
- Lease 34, 36-38, 44, 45, 229
- Mortgage 35
- New 68
- Owning 36, 229
- Set Asides 35

Landing or Log Decks 96-97
Legumes 201, 202
Licking Branches 151, 152, 162, 164, 165
Lime 17, 33, 43, 64, 83, 88, 90-92, 94, 97, 134, 136, 138-140, 158, 170, 175, 187, 202
Lignin 193, 194
Living Brush Pile 60-61
Logging 42, 96, 97, 123-126, 128-130, 230
  Performance Bond 130
  Skidders 88, 128-129
Logging Roads 14, 87-90, 92-96, 98, 99, 129, 130, 176, 179

M

Mast Producing Trees 40, 118-119
Monroe Tufline 89, 90, 143, 178

Mossy Oak 20, 194
Mowing 98, 146, 158, 179, 181, 187

N

New Zealand 175, 193, 194
Nitrogen Fixation 201-202
Northern Demo Center 15, 175
Nutrients 54, 64, 95, 115, 146, 191, 198, 200-204, 213

P

People Habitat 56, 113-114
Perennials 190, 191, 203, 166
Permission Hunting 68, 77, 79
pH 88, 139-140, 203
pH Meter 92
pHFertilizer 139-140
Planted Log Road 89
PlotMaster 17, 89, 90, 144
Posting 67-74, 180, 182
Posted Signs 72
  Aluminum Signs 67
  Paper Signs 72
Posting Guide Lines 73
Posting Property 44, 77

Q

Quality Deer Habitat 16, 29, 31-32, 51, 58, 121, 219
Quality Deer Hunting 16-18, 25, 29, 47, 68, 109, 207-223, 225, 226, 229, 230
Quality Deer Management 207, 209, 210, 220, 221
Quality Deer Management Association 209, 220, 222
Quality Whitetails 209, 222

R

Rain 142, 144, 147, 196
Regeneration 54, 56, 62, 64, 94, 113, 123, 170, 181

Index

Rick Bass 217
Rye Grass 94, 199

S

Sanctuary 13, 17, 101-109, 218
   Locating Sanctuaries 104
   Off-Limits Sanctuary 81, 101, 104, 107-109, 139
   Working Sanctuary 101, 105, 109
Secondary Roads & Trails 84
Security 39, 69, 76, 79
Security Cameras 81
Seed 33, 88, 91, 93, 95, 97, 141-144, 176, 179, 182, 183, 184, 192, 194, 195, 202-205
Seminars 17-18, 24, 45
Site Evaluations 38-39, 225-226
Soil Sample 92, 138-139, 175
Steuben County 13, 15, 36
Succession 63

T

Timber 35, 49, 56-57, 59, 88, 94, 113, 123-128, 130
Tours 16, 29, 85
Treepak 120
Trespasser 17, 44, 45, 67-82, 103
   Prosecuting Trespassers 74, 77-78
Timber Stand Improvement (TSI) 111-115

U

Utilization Cages 144-145

V

Venison Donation Coalition 211

W

Weed 179, 181, 182, 195
Windfloaters 153, 156
Woods, Dr. Grant 19-23, 182, 189
Written Plan 45, 47, 172, 226
www.mossyoakbiologic.com 205
www.NorthCountryWhitetails.com 205

Photo by Charles J. Alsheimer

Notes

Notes

Notes

Notes

Notes

Notes

Notes

Notes

Notes

GIVE THE GIFT OF
Grow 'Em Right
A Guide To Creating Habitat and Food Plots

To Your Hunting Firends, Club Members and Local Library.

❏ YES, I want _____ copies of *Grow 'Em Right, A Guide to Creating Habitat and Food Plots* for $19.95 each.

❏ YES, I am interested in having Neil Dougherty speak or give a seminar to my organization. Please send information.

   Include $5.05 shipping and handling for one book, and $2.00 for each additional book. New York residents must include applicable sales tax. Canadian orders must include payment in US funds.

Payment must accompany order. Allow 3 weeks for delivery.

My check or money order for $ _____ is enclosed.
Please charge my   ❏ Visa   ❏ MasterCard   ❏ Discover

Name _____
Organization _____
Address _____
City/State/Zip _____
Phone _____ Email _____
Card # _____
Exp. Date _____
Signature _____

For Faster Service
CALL or FAX **585-388-6990**
Or Order online at
www.NorthCountryWhitetails.com